WHAT READ~~ERS HAVE SAID~~

"This book should be in the hand of every middle age pastor. It will guide him as he recognizes his mortality as well as the dream that his work will not be in vain. Because of the smooth transition between Moses and Joshua, Moses became more powerful in his death than in his living."

EDWIN S. HARPER UBI DD THD,
BISHOP/PASTOR OF APOSTOLIC LIFE
CATHEDRAL IN HUNTINGTON, WV 35TH YEAR

"Transitions can be both challenging and intimidating. However, change also offers tremendous opportunities for growth. So, how does one ascertain the positives and avoid the negatives? Success often hinges on knowledge. Backed with scriptural principles, Robert Mitchell, in *The Truth About Succeeding in Ministry Transitions*, shares personal experiences as well as keen insights from mentors that can help anyone dealing with the uncertainty of change. The question is not, 'Will you experience a transition?' The question is, 'How well will you transition?' Robert Mitchell shares how to transition the right way."

DR. EUGENE WILSON, AUTHOR, SPEAKER,
ADJUNCT PROFESSOR, EXECUTIVE PASTOR,
AND FOUNDER OF EQUIPPING LEADERS

"A message that should be addressed more within the church for ministers coming or going through transitions; and Robert Mitchell exceptionally conveys that message in this book."

STEPHEN H. NEWTON, YOUTH PASTOR OF 4:12 YOUTH MINISTRIES OUT OF NEW LIFE PRAISE CENTER IN SEABROOK, TX

"As one who has went through transition with my father and watched as my dad handled it to perfection, I am always pulling for others to see the same results that I experienced. I said that to say that I fully believe that this book will be a huge key in helping you take that much needed step. Thank you, Pastor Mitchell, for putting the time and effort into writing this book."

AUTHOR/PASTOR DEE JAY SHOULDERS, FIRST APOSTOLIC CHURCH IN NASHVILLE, TN

"A very well detailed road map that will minimize taking the wrong path that can lead to hurt and wrecking relationships. If you are in the season of life that is facing a transition, I recommend this book as a guide to help you find the right path to follow."

ROY BARNHILL, PASTOR & BISHOP AT THE PENTECOSTALS OF LUMBERTON, NC FOR 40 YEARS

"Transitions are difficult in life. Any time there is movement outside of the comfort zones we have created in our lives, there tends to be doubt, stress, uncertainty and often times anxiety as to what is next. In this book you are introduced to not just a plan on how to transition, and do it correctly but insight into the murky waters of change by someone who has been down this road a time or two. Having faced ministerial transitions myself, often times doing so incorrectly, I found Robert's clarity on this matter to be a much needed resource for anyone who may be in the midst of a transition or looking into the face of change in the near distant future. This resource should be made available to every young minister involved in ministry or anyone even thinking about stepping into vast chasm of leadership in the church world. I cannot recommend this book strongly enough! By reading this book I am convinced one can avoid many pitfalls that often come during times of transition and change. Thank you Robert for providing this necessary and much needed resource."

AUTHOR/PASTOR DARIN SARGENT, THE POINT CHURCH IN ESCONDIDO, CA

"*The Truth About Succeeding in Ministry Transitions* is a must read to the soul that is searching for answers concerning the next step in ministry. To anyone who is presently in or entering a transition, this spiritual and practical insight is for you."

J. KURTIS BURTON, PASTOR, THE TURNING POINT IN NASHVILLE, TN

"Pastor Robert Mitchell has done it again! In *The Truth About Succeeding In Ministry Transitions*, Robert rips the band-aid off to expose the realities that anyone planning or going through a ministry transition must deal with. Having served in ministry for 25+ years and finding myself in a welcomed, but major ministry transition, I hoped my years of experience would naturally provide the answers I would need to succeed — it turns out I didn't even know the questions! Reading this book has both encouraged me through Robert's personal experiences and equipped me with his shared practical wisdom and provided steps for success. This book is a must have resource for every minister's library!"

DARRYL W. HOOPER, SENIOR PASTOR OF THE
CHURCH COVINGTON IN COVINGTON,
GEORGIA

"I've seen so many leadership transitions go bad! Thriving churches have suffered and souls have even been lost because of poor transitions. Why? Simply because there are not many people who have experience with transition. Lack of experience has caused transitional train wrecks. But now there is a voice of experience, author Robert Mitchell has been through the ups and downs of transition, and through it all, now he can be a voice of wisdom."

CHAD J ERICKSON, ASSOCIATE AND
ADMINISTRATIVE PASTOR FIRST APOSTOLIC
CHURCH OF MARYVILLE, TN

THE TRUTH ABOUT SUCCEEDING IN MINISTRY TRANSITIONS

WHAT EVERY MINISTER AND CHURCH GOER
FACING CHANGE NEEDS TO KNOW

ROBERT MITCHELL

ISBN: 9781710248029

NOTE TO THE READER

The Publisher/Author does not warrant or guarantee any of the products described herein or perform any independent analysis in connection with any of the product information contained herein. The publisher/author does not assume, and expressly disclaims, any obligation to obtain and include information other than that provided to it by the manufacturer. The reader is expressly warned to consider and adopt all safety precautions that might be indicated by the activities described herein and to avoid all potential hazards. By following the instructions contained herein, the reader willingly assumes all risks in connection with such instructions. The publisher/author makes no representations or warranties of any kind, including but not limited to, the warranties of fitness for particular purpose or merchantability, nor are any such representations implied with respect to the material set forth herein, and the publisher/author takes no responsibility with respect to such material. The publisher/author shall not be liable for any special, consequential, or exemplary damages resulting, in whole or part, from the readers' use of, or reliance upon, this material.

Disclaimer: The information provided in this book should not be substituted for, or used to alter, therapy without your doctor's advice. For specific health problems, consult your physician. Mention of specific authors, companies, products, or organizations does not necessarily imply endorsement by the author, nor does mention of specific authors, companies, products, or organizations imply that they endorse the book or author.

To the memory of the greatest man I've ever known, my father. My premier privilege is to carry his name. To me, he could accomplish anything. He left his mark on the world, pushed the Kingdom of God forward, blessed humanity with no reserve, and departed into eternity "Unique—not Antique."

And to my father-in-law, who has imparted unparalleled wisdom into my life over the past 30 years. His most generous act was allowing me to marry his youngest daughter. She is my everything and has provided for us three priceless treasures: our children. Lisa, I love you!

CONTENTS

FOREWORD

I first met Rev. Robert Mitchell in the 1980's, when he and a minister friend held a revival for us in Stockton, CA at Christian Life Center. I knew him as "Robbie" back then. Bishop Kenneth Haney and I were friends with his parents; his father had held revivals for us and blessed our church. We love their family.

Robbie Mitchell has evangelized, been a pastor and has worked with his lovely wife, as a Home Missionary, while growing a thriving church in Colorado. He's done many things and now is releasing a new book that God has inspired him to write. It will be important and vital for every minister to have this book in their library! The title is *"The TRUTH about Succeeding in Ministry TRANSITIONS."*

He introduces the book with this statement: "Change is an intricate part of human existence. Before we can move forward, into all the potential that life can afford, we have to accept that fact. Some of life's greatest hindrances come from our feeble attempts to avoid anything other than what is common or ordinary to us. As a minister, I think my main responsibility is to stay sensitive to the direction of God's Spirit, follow after His leading, and somehow not lose my way in the midst of the coming changes – which, for those who are involved, can be overwhelming. Both the minister and the church members are affected in times of transition."

This book is peppered throughout with rich insights from some of the great elders who have passed on, as well as students of the Word, whom God has raised up in this generation, to be well-respected teachers.

He weaves, very skillfully, the story of ministerial transition, using illustrations and real-life stories, and sheds light on all the subjects that need to be addressed! He includes Biblical characters, minister friends, other authors, and interesting facts. It will be a gold mine of excellent advice and proper legal procedures to follow, step-by-step, for the outgoing pastor, the incoming pastor, and the church.

It's a beautiful book, with excellent material, written by a sincere man of God to bless the ministers working in God's Kingdom!

—Joy Haney

Prolific writer and speaker, Joy Haney, author of over 60 books, served as First Lady of Christian Life Center in Stockton, California for 30 years and First Lady of the United Pentecostal Church, International for 8 years, while her husband, Bishop Kenneth Haney was General Superintendent. Sister Haney has also ministered throughout North America and around the world.

http://JoylHaney.com

I

INTRODUCTION

NO PLAN B

AS A CHAPLAIN with the Aurora (Colorado) Police Department, I was recently honored to offer an invocation at a Law Enforcement Torch Run (LETR) International Conference for Special Olympics.

Leading up to the event, there was a preliminary, face-to-face meeting with the Colorado (LETR) Vice President to cover expectations, followed by multiple emails, spelling out the details. When I accepted the invitation, I had no idea how big the event was or the responsibility I would feel. I arrived early, met my escort, was handed a packet of credentials, and quickly taken backstage where I got to see what happens behind the scenes.

With 1,100 people in attendance from 48 states, Canadian Provinces, and many different countries, everything was on a strict timeline and the pressure was on. After being given all the details, I was fully prepared to step from behind the curtains when it was my time. First, though, there would be the revered Olympic Torch ceremony followed by an introduction of my name through the sound system, then I was instructed to cross the stage, adjust the microphone to my chin, and speak.

As my time approached, a program director continually informed me of the countdown starting with 15 minutes, then ten minutes, then five minutes, then three minutes. During those moments, the representative torch was being ceremonially placed on a designated stand beside the podium and I was patiently waiting for my moment.

Then, I was momentarily distracted from the countdown when I noticed a stagehand near me. He was holding a container with an additional flame. That seemed odd to me and I learned that his flame was an extra one, in case the "real" one burned out, for some reason. Thankfully, the extra flame wasn't ultimately needed, and the event went off without a hitch, except that my carefully-crafted notes mysterious disappeared the moment I started to speak! But I'll save that story for another time.

Back-up plans are always a good idea, especially when a blunder could potentially affect many people, but when it comes to a ministry transition, there typically isn't a Plan B. No one is standing backstage, ready to relight the torch if it goes out. It's important to get it right the first time.

CHANGE IS COMING, READY OR NOT

CHANGE IS INEVITABLE. Many individuals live their lives as though this reality is some unfounded, unrealistic, unheard-of truth. Time and time again in the areas of science, discovery, health, and exploration it has been proven that anything living is changing.

Change is an intricate part of human existence. Before we can move forward, into all the potential that life can afford, we have to accept that fact. Some of life's greatest hindrances come from our feeble attempts to avoid anything other than what is common or ordinary to us.

We like our routine and thrive in its structure. We don't generally like change, even though, in many circumstances, it may be the very thing we need, to arrive at a better place in our life. Let's settle the fact that change is inevitable. If we can prepare ourselves for that reality now, then when life takes its unexpected turns, we won't be so negatively affected.

Change is going to happen. Even to ministers and their families.

In some cases, it's an older minister who needs to step back from the heavy load of pastoral responsibility. Sometimes it's a younger minister, stepping into a bigger ministry responsibility. And, always, with all ministerial transitions, change also happens to the people who are ministered to, by those leaders.

Sometimes change is sudden, as with a death. Other times, every detail is carefully-planned in advance. Either way, when the transitions happen, how much better is it when we know that, at some point, change is coming. And, if it's a new experience for us, we don't really know what's normal and how to make it through. We don't know what we don't know!

As John C. Maxwell says, "As long as a person doesn't know what he doesn't know, he doesn't grow." This book will serve as a resource for all those affected by ministerial transitions.

Ministerial transitions will come to each person who is involved in the process of a gospel mandate. As Maxwell points out in his book, *The 21 Irrefutable Laws of Leadership*, not knowing what we don't know, is the first of four phases of leadership growth and it falls under the heading of "The Law of Process."

What you don't know shouldn't keep you from moving forward, once you do know. Don't allow yourself the mistake of being clueless about ministry change because, trust me, change is coming and, in all honesty, the right change can be a good thing.

I encourage you to be convinced of, and comfortable with, the necessity and reality of change. Transition will happen, whether you like it, want it, or not! As a minister, I settled the fact long ago; there is no benefit in wasting energy trying to avoid transition. If you try, the outcome is never good. Welcome what is coming, as part of the Lord's ideal course for your future. Simply put, His decisions are always what's best.

Remove whatever doubt you have about this truth. You can't live out your purpose without experiencing continual personal shifts, and once you've accepted this, be aligned with its necessity. Transition and change must happen for individual growth and kingdom advancement to occur. It's reality.

Unfortunately, we don't always get these transitions right. While there are moments when we are simply overwhelmed and doubt that anything productive is happening, don't make ministry transitions more difficult than they have to be! Face each one with clarity, information, assurance, and owned directives. Then, you can be confident about the outcome.

From my perspective, what stops people in ministry from moving forward is often fear. They've heard the stories of others' tragic outcomes and the trouble and unnecessary difficulties that resulted from their attempt to remain obedient to a higher expectation. And many folks have heard more negative than positive examples, like we hear in the current challenging political landscape, which is filled with false narratives, negative reporting, and fake news. It's difficult to weed through the insatiable amount of press to uncover the truth.

But, it's like anything else. Trouble always seems to get more airplay than the triumph. When people discuss ministry transitions, they're often speaking from a negative experience, or from some tragic outcome, and the focus is on the difficulty they faced. When someone endures, survives, and, ultimately flourishes in those overwhelming situations, it's commendable. But in reality, the stories of fallout and loss get the most attention and ignite the most fear.

Family members, friends, and even strangers have shared horror stories about ministry transitions. The ironic part is, we automatically gravitate toward thoughts and feelings of pessimism and find it all but impossible to process our transitions any other way. Be careful not to "naturally" internalize someone else's struggle, when the situation you're facing has a completely different set of circumstances.

Be reassured that digging a little deeper can reveal that victories in the area of ministry transitions do happen on a regular basis. Good things do happen in times of leadership change, but it seems, when you're in the middle of things and the pressure is on, you have to work harder to find them.

So, don't just consider the fearful stories and the tragic outcomes when you face a transition. Those stories stop some people, but there's a way through the transition, if you learn what to expect, know how to process it, and have a plan for what to do in these moments. If you know what to expect, you'll have a plan internalized before the challenges arrive.

This book will provide helpful insights to help you thrive—even through stress-filled ministerial changes.

YOU'LL PROBABLY SURVIVE THE TRANSITION

I AM in my sixth decade of life and my third decade of ministry, so I've been through many major ministry transitions. The important thing is, I'm still here to talk about it, so I guess you could say that I'm a survivor. I haven't lost my faith in God, my perspective of the kingdom, or my confidence in God-called leaders. Many others, in similar circumstances, can't say the same.

Through the years, I have personally witnessed an untold number of people, both in the ministry and not, lose their way as a result of ministry transitions. It's sad, but not everyone navigates through the years of the uncertainties of ministry. I hope this book will help mitigate some of those losses.

I understand that addressing an unpopular issue is bold, but these situations don't just work themselves out. Being successful in times of ministerial change can take a long time to really figure out.

In navigating through ministry change, my personal experiences have been basically good, but not without challenges. As a minister, I think my main responsibility is to stay sensitive to the direction of

God's Spirit, follow after His leading, and somehow not lose my way in the midst of the coming changes—which, for those who are involved, can be overwhelming.

One of the most valuable lessons I've learned as it relates to this subject is transitions designed and inspired by God are much bigger than just me. Change affects many people. It's like the long cast of a shadow on a summer evening. An enormous amount of landscape is touched. The plan and uniqueness of the call of God on an individual's life, along with the destiny of a church congregation, is more extensive and far-reaching than one could even start to comprehend.

It's so important to carefully consider both those in the pulpit and those in the pew when working through ministry transitions. No one in the picture escapes. The challenge is not an isolated challenge. Everyone involved feels the stress. The work of the kingdom is bigger than you and me!

Both the minister and the church members are affected in times of transition. Although the primary focus of this book is directed toward the minister, anyone who reads it will be able to see behind the thick, alienating curtain, often considered "off limits," even if it's in a small way, and hopefully, better understand some of the moving parts that are not always obvious during these times of change.

But it's not just the faithful church members and pastor who are affected. Anyone who has any sort of connection to the church are touched by these major transitions, including the minister's family, employed and volunteer staff members, occasional church attenders, those who formerly attended the church, and even the community. And they all matter. That's why it's so important to consider all the factors and all the people when undertaking a ministerial transition. It's vitally important to get it right, even in times of uncertainty.

WHAT ABOUT THE PEOPLE?

I'M thankful every ministry transition doesn't end up being a negative thing. In fact, they should end up being positive and productive, in most—if not all—situations. The key is approaching major change the right way.

How do you do that? By stripping all of the challenges away and remembering the most important question: "What about the people?" Many ministerial transitions are attempted without truthfully considering what's best for the congregation and its future.

Ministers should realize first and foremost, that those who make up the local congregation are not "your" people. They don't belong to you, so, I emphatically suggest, you stop taking ownership. The church is His heritage, it's not the pastor's, an organization's, or a denomination's.

1 Peter 5:1-4 declares, *"The elders which are among you I exhort, who am also an elder, and a witness of the sufferings of Christ, and also a partaker of the glory that shall be revealed: Feed the flock of*

God which is among you, taking the oversight thereof, not by constraint, but willingly; not for filthy lucre, but of a ready mind; Neither as being lords over God's heritage, but being examples to the flock. And when the chief Shepherd shall appear, ye shall receive a crown of glory that fadeth not away."

He is the shepherd, and we, as ministers, need to be reminded from time to time, that we're only under-shepherds. God gives the church pastors according to His heart, as the Old Testament mentions in Jeremiah 3:15, *"And I will give you pastors according to mine heart, which shall feed you with knowledge and understanding.*

Once again, there is a vast difference between ownership and oversight. We take too much ownership on ourselves when we carelessly do what we want to do, without considering what God thinks is best—for not only the church but our own lives.

NO NEED TO WALK THIS ROAD ALONE

I SPENT many years in the pursuit of education, and earned a couple of college degrees; however, the real challenge came when it was time to apply all that acquired knowledge.

Truthfully, the lion's share of what I've learned about successful ministerial transitions definitely came on-the-job. One of the main reasons I feel motivated to address the issue of ministerial transition is because I want people to have the opportunity to hear it, experience it, and see it from someone else's reality.

This, in many ways, is our best ally. No need to reinvent the wheel or to learn the hard way.

It's hard for some ministers to be vulnerable and humble enough to ask for help when they need it. We would rather try to handle life on our own, but the truth is, everyone will need help at some point. We need people around us who can advise us and come to our rescue when necessary. It's not always easy to take others' advice to heart, because that means we're admitting we don't have it all figured out.

Trying to traverse this road of transition alone is asking for a tragic outcome or a tumultuous journey, at best. Early in scripture, Genesis 2:18 reveals, *"And the Lord God said, It is not good that the man should be alone; I will make him an help meet for him."* From the beginning, God showed us that attempting life alone isn't the most opportune design.

Later in scripture, we find this warning, *"Two are better than one; because they have a good reward for their labour. For if they fall, the one will lift up his fellow: but woe to him that is alone when he falleth; for he hath not another to help him up."* Ecclesiastes 4:9-10

I emphatically maintain that "alone" is not the way to tackle ministry transitions—not for the minister or for the saint. For one thing, what may have worked in a specific area of the country or world, or in a particular church doesn't necessarily work in another location, congregation, or cultural setting. Instead of allowing yourself to become exhausted, discouraged and frustrated, trying to press through, whatever it costs, why not swallow your pride, refuse to allow personal ego to interfere, be vulnerable, and ask for help?

It's imperative to remove the secrecy that tends to dominate times like these and make solid choices on what can be disclosed to fellow ministers and the church family and what should be kept private. And once you make the decision, stick with it.

I've experienced many strong direct and indirect successful voices in my life. These voices came in the form of family, friends, and others I intentionally sought out over the years. There's no way I can name them all! But a few, however, must be mentioned.

The first and most valuable mentor was my own father, Robert L. Mitchell. My observation of his life and the many conversations we had concerning ministry helped shape the landscape of success for me. No other individual can equal his example in my life and that's why I've chosen to reference him so much in this book.

Second, in my mid-twenties, I married into a family of transitional ministry success. Immediately, my father-in-law, Johnny P. Godair became a wealth of knowledge to me and at this point of my life, he's my closest confidant. His exemplary life, biblical knowledge, pastoral experience, kingdom passion, and the countless times he communicated his personal journey, have benefited me immeasurably.

I consider myself blessed because of these two men and their incalculable investments in my life.

I believe, with mentors, you have to respect their advice, even though you may not always understand or even agree with it. A personal principle I live by is, why do things the difficult way?

Consider the advice of trusted others as an important opportunity to learn, instead of being forced to acquire the knowledge the hard way. You can gain invaluable assets for direction in life, both with the menial tasks and the major responsibilities.

There's unlimited help to be garnered, because they have walked the road before you. It's wise to take advantage of their advice; it does help immensely with the on-the-job training challenges. Take advantage of the opportunities offered to you and utilize them to build upon someone else's experience. There's so much strength from one generation to the next.

While navigating transition, continually seek counsel from those who understand the unique situation you are facing. Reach out to those who've experienced a similar type of circumstance, whether in a numerically large or a small church setting. The need for outside and unbiased contributions cannot be overstated. We need to rely on those people in all of our lives who understand the intricate calling we possess and how God gives every minister a different set of responsibilities.

On a side note—regarding today's plethora of possibilities online, you might find a few resources that can help with some aspects of the transitional process, but it is limited. The absolute best help will come from trusted confidants, who have successfully journeyed though similar circumstances. Don't be afraid to lean on them. What is new to you may be old hat for them. Find individuals who are unbiased and willing to share openly with you and be transparent and honest with them. Let them walk with you, through the challenges of the transition.

If you possess clarity in your calling, understanding of your mission, and make decisions based on how they will enhance the kingdom of God, that will help you find the right answers and the right people to learn from, through the process. We should never lose sight of the sobering fact that souls, along with the future growth, (both numerically and spiritually), and the prosperity of the congregation, is what ultimately matters.

Pastoral "on-the-job training" can be demoralizing, yet, that's exactly where many ministers find themselves. The abundance of sad stories concerning congregants and ministers who didn't make it through their first major pastoral shake-up, is staggering.

I know some, in both the pulpit and the pew, who lost everything of value in their life. They lost their companions, children, and material possessions, as well as their ministries. Churches were destroyed and influence was decimated, not only in the church family and its connections, but also in the surrounding community. Friends, dreams, ambitions, livelihoods, everything was just lost in the midst of trying to get through a ministerial transition. Some even lost their souls.

Many won't admit it, but the ministry and church life can be an unforgiving business. The sad reality is, way too many people don't learn this until they're in the middle of their challenge.

Ideally, a ministerial transition would be clean, planned out, and perfect, with all the details falling into place according to God's perfect will. Wouldn't that be nice? We'd also like all the stars to align, concerning our circumstances. But the truth is, sometimes you're thrust into situations out of obligated necessity and, not only are you unaware of how you got there, you're also oblivious about how you're going to make it through!

By the grace of God, some survive and are able to look back, and say, "I have no answer on how we made it through. But, thank God, we were one of the fortunate ones who endured!" Surety is elusive at best, when we operate simply out of the flesh.

It's so important to talk candidly about these things so those who are coming along behind will understand that they're not an anomaly. These things are a reality for most ministers at some time in their ministry.

When you're thrown into the deep end, you either sink or swim. I know that from personal experience! I learned to swim quite young, when my late father threw me into the deep end of a Holiday Inn pool in Texarkana, Texas. A couple of modern day floaties, an old orange yoke lifejacket, or noodle would have been nice! I find the memory amusing now, because I survived it, but it wasn't funny at all, when it was happening. By the way, I ended up earning a PhD in dog paddling, although I'm probably scarred for life! By the way, all three of my daughters were taught to swim by an experienced teacher who assisted them through every step of the process.

In all seriousness, that moment when someone has to let go of their previous responsibility and take hold of the next one is critical. Ministries—and the Kingdom—are enhanced or lost in those times. Every decision must be made carefully, understanding this reality. No matter how promising or bright the new situation looks, or how anxious the departing one is, to go, don't neglect the importance of the details of the transition.

The best of transitions will always involve others, including advisors, mentors, boards, peers—even family. And, without question, the minister's spouse must be abundantly clear on whatever the arrangements are and kept in the loop on the decisions being made. Secrecy breeds many unnecessary questions, assumptions, and unfounded fears.

II

WHAT DOES THE BIBLE SAY ABOUT MINISTERIAL TRANSITIONS?

ROADBLOCKS

THERE IS no greater roadblock in ministry transition than the absence of a specific scriptural example to cover the different aspects, conditions, uniqueness, and possibilities of the situation. Unfortunately, for those who would prefer a list of "Thou Shalts" or "Thou Shalt Nots" concerning pastoral transitions, they're going to be disappointed because there are no rigid or set processes laid out for the early church. So, since the New Testament doesn't provide a detailed template to follow, we have to start the discussion by realizing that there's no real right or wrong way to transition from one pastor to another.

I asked my friend, Raymond Woodward, who pastors in Fredericton, New Brunswick Canada, an astute student of scripture about this reality of scripture. He said:

> I don't know if there's a clear process in the New Testament. I think there's a clear pattern, and in my opinion, too often in our fellowship, more specifically, the apostolic church, we see a pattern that says, "I must die, so that he can live, or lead." But I

think the Biblical pattern is John the Baptist saying, "I must decrease, so that he can increase." Decreasing seems to be much harder than dying for most leaders—especially, when it means that someone else is increasing at the same time. We don't do that well, as ministers. It's hard to purposefully decrease while someone else is increasing. It's easier to think that we have to die before someone else can lead.

He isn't the only pastor I know who shares this perspective. I'll highlight another in a later chapter.

In all sincerity, I've repeatedly observed this way of thinking throughout my ministry, and I'm convinced this is not just the perspective of a few, but the concrete opinion of many. Unfortunately, too many well-meaning, misinformed, otherwise effective leaders, have perished on that "death over decrease" mountain instead of considering the kingdom. They would rather perish than relinquish control. And that perspective negatively affects all those who are connected to the church.

A more enlightened consideration would come by understanding the individual calling alongside the reality that God assigns different ministry responsibilities for different seasons. Timing is critically important throughout the life of the minister.

PREDICTABILITY GOES HAND-IN-HAND WITH UNPREDICTABILITY— MOSES AND JOSHUA

WHILE WE DON'T HAVE a specific, step-by-step plan to follow for ministerial transitions, there are a couple of stories in the scripture to glean from.

A premier Bible story of leadership transition is the one detailed between Moses and Joshua. This change is happening in the life of, perhaps, the greatest leader in scripture, outside of Jesus Christ. Notice that the transition took place from one individual to another individual, one leader to the next leader, not church to church, or congregation to congregation. And God told Moses exactly what to do.

In Deuteronomy 3:23-28, God tells Moses how to transition the leadership to Joshua and how to treat the younger man:

"And I [Moses] besought the Lord at that time, saying, O Lord God, thou hast begun to shew thy servant thy greatness, and thy mighty hand: for what God is there in heaven or in earth, that can do according to thy works, and according to thy might? I pray thee, let me go over, and see the good land that is beyond Jordan, that goodly

mountain, and Lebanon. But the Lord was wroth with me for your sakes, and would not hear me: and the Lord said unto me, Let it suffice thee; speak no more unto me of this matter. Get thee up into the top of Pisgah, and lift up thine eyes westward, and northward, and southward, and eastward, and behold it with thine eyes: for thou shalt not go over this Jordan."

Read these next few words carefully...

"But charge Joshua, and encourage him, and strengthen him: for he shall go over before this people, and he shall cause them to inherit the land which thou shalt see."

This section of scripture is rich with insight. What Moses finally heard from God, when he wanted to continue to lead was, *"speak no more unto me of this matter."* God was telling Moses that it was time for a transition to new leadership. Basically, God was telling him "just do what I'm requiring you to do"—which was to step back and let the next generation take the main leadership position. There will come a moment when Heaven will say to each minister, "You've gone as far as I will permit."

That doesn't mean we don't have additional responsibilities. We do. God just expects different things for our lives. God didn't intend for Joshua to travel this time of change by himself. Moses was right there for the transition, making sure Joshua was ready.

This, learn-on-your-own, earn-your-own-respect mentality, which I've seen displayed towards the next generation, by many seasoned, and I dare say, jaded leaders, has no place in ministry transition. Moses was required to not only charge Joshua, but to also encourage and strengthen him. Part of a healthy transfer includes support and care from the retiring minister to the new leader, who really needs it, given the responsibility the new leader will soon shoulder.

For Joshua it was leading the people and literally, making a way for them to possess their long-awaited promises. What an enormous task he faced! Often God expects more from the next generation than the previous.

The Moses and Joshua transition is a prime example of Moses making the conscious choice, with God's direction, to decrease while Joshua was increasing. He could have died while trying to hold onto the past. Instead, he accepted God's directive of the inevitable transition. An interesting side-note is no spouse was mentioned in this transition at all, even though this had to be one of the most difficult types of situations for those leaders and their spouses to encounter.

To understand what was promoting this transition, we should start in Numbers 27:14, where God told Moses, *"For ye rebelled against my commandment in the Desert of Zin, in the strife of the congregation, to sanctify me at the water before their eyes, that is in the water of Meribah in Kadesh in the wilderness of Zin."*

God was referring to a particular rebellion from Moses in the past. That rebellion limited Moses from fulfilling the plan for his future leadership. Even though Moses wanted to continue, the poor decisions made early in his leadership short-circuited his larger desire. It's so important to make right choices early in the process of leading. Measure the chances and choices by tight criteria, fully understanding the inescapable future consequences.

What resulted for Moses was an example of a leader wanting to hold on beyond his purpose and him trying to lead when it was no longer his responsibility. He needed to make a transition and God revealed to Moses who it should be and how it should happen. It's dangerous for people to get caught up in what's happening and miss what God is wanting. When He's ready for a pastoral change, the leader needs to let go instead of holding on.

At times, distractions will come to leaders in the midst of decisions, and judgment will also come on those who do not represent God correctly. This is what we see in Numbers 27:14. There is visible rebellion against God's commandment in the desert, which caused strife within the congregation. As a result, God said, *"Sanctify me at the water before their eyes."* When this didn't happen, judgment came.

Once Moses accepted that his time of leading was ending, at least in that particular capacity, his first concern was for the welfare of the people he'd been leading. He spoke to the Lord, in verses 15-17, and asked, *"...the* LORD, *the God of the spirits of all flesh, set a man over the congregation, which may go out before them, and which may go in before them, and which may lead them out, and which may bring them in; that the congregation of the* LORD *be not as sheep which have no shepherd."*

He's sincerely requesting, "If this current challenge means I'm not going to be able to go forward as the leader, then, please, raise someone up who can lead, because the people need a shepherd."

In response, the Lord directed Moses in verses 18-23 to *"...Take thee Joshua the son of Nun, a man in whom is the spirit, and lay thine hand upon him; and set him before Eleazar the priest, and before all the congregation; and give him a charge in their sight. And thou shalt put some of thine honour upon him, that all the congregation of the children of Israel may be obedient. And he shall stand before Eleazar the priest, who shall ask counsel for him after the judgment of Urim before the* LORD: *at his word shall they go out, and at his word they shall come in, both he, and all the children of Israel with him, even all the congregation. And Moses did as the* LORD *commanded him: and he took Joshua, and set him before Eleazar the priest, and before all the congregation: and he laid his hands upon him, and gave him a charge, as the* LORD *commanded by the hand of Moses."*

This time when the commandment came, Moses obeyed

completely, even though he would have preferred to be the one to remain in the position and he did exactly what God instructed him to do. A transition like this requires the leader to totally abandon self and completely trust in the sovereignty of God.

The direction Moses received was *"put some of your honor on him."* The people cannot be without a leader and since you're not going one step farther, make sure there's a plan and person for the future leadership.

It is absolutely imperative that we notice—and follow, in our own lives—the details coming from God. Even though he wasn't allowed either the choice to move aside or to decide who the next leader would be, Moses had to make every attempt to secure the place of leadership for Joshua in the people's eyes.

Working against or tearing down the next leader doesn't benefit the exiting leader or bless the people of God in any way. Joshua wasn't begging for the position, and neither was Moses asking God to pick Joshua. But once God laid out the plan for the future, Moses followed it. He intentionally commissioned Joshua, transferring the authority, direction and approval to him.

The concept and desire of *"they must not be left without a shepherd"* tells us that, in God's eyes, and in the eyes of true, God-honoring leaders, the people matter!

Joshua became the one who cared for the people, and who led them, and his word and decisions were to take effect, immediately. What's interesting is in the following few chapters, even though Joshua was made the commissioned leader in Numbers 27, Moses was still giving commands, after their transition before the people. This is a great example of proper leadership transfer. The ongoing connection of Moses, the former leader, to the new leader, was key.

THE BENEFIT OF A FRONT ROW SEAT—PAUL AND TIMOTHY

AN ADDITIONAL BIBLICAL example of ministerial transition is found in the New Testament, regarding Paul and his relationships with those he mentored and passed ministry roles to. They're telling, especially the one he had with Timothy.

Others have referenced this dynamic relationship in detail and revealed tremendous insight and explanation, so my consideration will be brief.

The influence of Paul started out in the form of a spiritual father-figure to Timothy, since the Bible mentions Timothy's father was a Greek, indicating he didn't have a male Christian example from his dad to draw from, as a child.

Paul calls Timothy, *"My own son in the faith."* (1 Timothy 1:2)

Then Timothy is invited and strategically given the opportunity to travel with the apostle on various missionary journeys, providing Timothy a front row seat to watch Paul and learn, by example, how to be an effective minister. I might add, this type of mentorship is recognizably absent in many leadership settings. Influence has its most effect, up close.

John Maxwell says, "A leader is one who knows the way, goes the way, and shows the way."

Finally, in the end, he calls Timothy a fellow-laborer, and, at this point they were more like equals or co-laborers. Although the Bible doesn't reveal every detail to us, we can assume, since he was younger than Paul, Timothy's ministry continued to move forward after Paul's was over.

Lee Grady contributing editor of *Charisma Magazine* said the Apostle Paul, who is a paramount model for ministry, made discipling the next generation his central focus. Acts 16:1-3 tells us about when he first met his disciple, Timothy, and how Timothy was eventually appointed as an apostolic leader in Ephesus.

"Then came he to Derbe and Lystra: and, behold, a certain disciple was there, named Timotheus, the son of a certain woman, which was a Jewess, and believed; but his father was a Greek: Which was well reported of by the brethren that were at Lystra and Iconium. Him would Paul have to go forth with him; and took and circumcised him because of the Jews which were in those quarters: for they knew all that his father was a Greek." Acts 16:1-3

Interestingly, one-third of the New Testament was either written to Timothy or written from Paul and Timothy. There are salutations mentioning Timothy in:

- 2 Corinthians 1:1 *"Paul, an apostle of Jesus Christ by the will of God, and Timothy our brother...,"*
- Philippians 1:1 *"Paul and Timotheus, the servants of Jesus Christ...,"*
- Colossians 1:1 *"Paul, an apostle of Jesus Christ by the will of God, and Timotheus our brother...,"*

- 1 Thessalonians 1:1, 2 Thessalonians 1:1 *"Paul, and Silvanus, and Timotheus, unto the church of the Thessalonians...,"*
- Philemon 1:1 *"Paul, a prisoner of Jesus Christ, and Timothy our brother..."*

Paul's investment in the next generation is reflected in the actual canon of scripture, yet we've overlooked the principle. Paul invested his life in Timothy, and he was so proud of him that he told the Philippians, *"I have no one else of kindred spirit who will genuinely be concerned for your welfare."* Philippians 2:20. (NASB) Then Paul added, *"But you know of his proven worth, that he served with me in the furtherance of the Gospel like a child serving his father."* (vs. 22).

This investment extended beyond just Timothy. Another epistle is addressed to Paul's young trainee, Titus, showing Paul's pattern of influence, but not necessarily a step by step requirement. Paul showed the importance of connections, time invested, confidence conferred, and spiritual direction.

Bishop L. Chancy Gore of The Refuge Church, Wylie, Texas, said, "Apostolic sons and daughters in the gospel are a must for the pastor and local church. Birthing, nurturing, raising, and releasing is a sacred trust. Helping Timothy, Titus and their wives find their place and callings is a sacred trust. It's a form of apostolic multiplication."

Both the Moses/Joshua and Paul/Timothy transitions were opportunities for the more mature leader to mentor the younger and to continue to be a voice of wisdom in their lives when they were attempting to lead on their own.

One of John Maxwell's Leadership Development concepts is about equipping the new leader for the job. An insightful explanation given on *How Leaders Develop* was in his blog on May 2, 2012:

Equipping begins with expectations. Namely, that leadership is influence, that leadership can be learned, and that leaders can multiply their influence by equipping others.

Equipping succeeds with training. Telling is not teaching, and listening is not learning. We learn to do by doing; training must be interactive.

Equipping continues with teaching. The reward of a teacher is a changed life. Success comes through achievement, but significance results from helping others to grow.

Practically speaking, the equipping process can be broken down into five steps.

- Say it: explain the task.
- Show it: demonstrate how to perform the task.
- Assign it: let the other person attempt the task.
- Study it: observe how the person performed the task.
- Assess it: offer feedback based on the person's performance.

With that said, what a huge opportunity it is for new leaders to stay close to the people who have already been there and done that, so they can be a mentor and help along the way. Remember, going alone, through a major transition, is not good.

Whether you're at the beginning or the end of your leadership responsibilities, always remember your place. If the timing is not right for you to start pastoring, or, if you've been the lead pastor for many years and now it's time to transition out of that position, be okay with it. Other opportunities which are beneficial to the kingdom, will present themselves during both stages of ministry.

Senior Pastor Ron Macey of Royalwood Church, Houston, Texas states, "Some people do not exit well from positions, offices, places of honor or stations of life. How we exit reveals who we really are. Anyone can step up on the stage of life; it's stepping down that spotlights true character. Exit well. Someone's watching."

An insightful suggestion, for the soon-to-be-replaced pastor, is to start working, well before the transition arrives, to find other ministerial responsibilities and fulfillment, besides preaching in the pulpit three times a week and handling the usual pastoral responsibilities. This may require becoming proactive about personal involvement in additional training, classes, and study. These self-imposed pursuits, along with other intentional activity, will help open up what might otherwise be improbable future opportunities.

Just remember that there is responsibility on both sides, from "the Paul" and "the Timothy," to wholeheartedly prioritize their relationship, understand each individual's role in the transition, and communicate with clarity.

CHARACTER AND INTEGRITY

MARTIN LUTHER KING, Jr. stated in his famous I Have A Dream speech, that people should be judged just by "the content of their character." That will go down in history as one of the most quoted phrases of any American speech. Several decades later, Peggy Noonan wrote a book about former United States President Ronald Reagan, and she titled it, "When Character Was King."

For a minister—especially one in the midst of a transition—character is the most vital component and should receive the most attention. In fact, outside of the will of God, nothing is more important than the character of those involved. It's so important that all parties have uncompromised integrity and the utmost trust of everyone potentially affected.

When Lisa and I were considering a move ministry from Asheville, North Carolina to Fayetteville, North Carolina, the unanimous feedback we received from the trusted advisors we confided in about this potential change, was that retiring pastor, Jesse Williams was, indeed, an ethical man of his word, and he could be trusted, without hesitation, to do exactly what he said he would do. My mentors, confidants and trusted friends, independently of each other, were all saying the same thing. I was entering into an agreement with a kingdom-minded man who possessed impeccable "character."

Even though Pastor Williams and I were separated by decades of age and experience, we shared a mutual ministerial respect. The respect I gave to him, he reciprocated back to me and vice-versa. He continually showed that respect. For instance, when I'd make decisions and changes early on as the new Senior Pastor of the church that he'd previously pastored, (and was now attending as a member of the congregation), some of the church members would approach him with questions or concerns. Without fail, even though he could have responded in any number of ways, over and over again, he'd direct them back to me, even though he was their former pastor.

His actions strengthened my authority, position, and confidence. This is what character looks like in a local church setting. It was an example of the Moses/Joshua scenario, *"put some of your honor on him."* And I quickly recognized this act of unwavering support from the greatest influencer in that church family. As a result, for the number of years I spent leading in that unique environment, I carefully measured every word and action in order to strengthen and not undermine his legacy.

As a new pastor, I was directing in different ways, and taking big risks, which I considered steps of faith, and, because he was there supporting me, I was able to lead in that manner with confidence. "My" success was built on his impeccable forty-year influence, especially until I could develop trust with the people myself. I readily admit that there is no good way to fulfill this calling of ministry alone.

After Jesse Williams passed away, his sweet supportive wife confirmed this to me while standing in front of his casket. She said her late husband knew I would stand by my word. I honestly felt the same way about him. There was a shared trust, stemming from unwavering character from the beginning or we would have never decided to go through the transition.

Pastor Williams was a man of his word, possessed the highest of integrity, operated with unquestionable character, displayed ministerial ethics and most of all was the finest of Christian examples. I miss his presence.

Our relationship was secure and continued that way throughout the remaining time we spent together. We both knew the transition was a critical season for the church and all the people involved. We had to get it right. Everything was hinging on the strong mutual respect he and I had for each other.

Although there was no direct or close connection between us, previous to me assuming the senior pastorate there, (outside of a few revival services years before when I'd evangelized and being a part of the same ministerial fellowship), he felt confident in me because of a direction from God, and distant observation over the years.

It is indicative of the similar example found in the New Testament examples. Our transition wasn't exactly like theirs, but there is a closely-connected principle.

The apostle Paul and his relationship with Timothy modeled before all, the importance of apostolic leaders carefully choosing and then investing in those who are younger and will follow them in ministry.

Previous growth experiences Lisa and I have enjoyed in ministry came elsewhere, but the fact that we were selected happened through Pastor Williams' sensitivity to the Lord and willingness to pass his labor on to the next generation.

The reality is a huge chance is taken by every leader feeling the direction to turn their labor of love over to another individual. Sometimes it proves to be the right move and in other situations it ends detrimentally. Having no Biblical mandate, the best way to overcome potential disaster is to rely heavily on character.

This is what kingdom trust looks like. This is mutual respect at its finest and most pure level. What kind of character and integrity do the parties contain and display? From my perspective, in the absence of a detailed Biblical plan or unalterable template to follow, nothing is more important. When it comes to potentially sticky ministerial transitions and situations, character will always count most!

III

PRACTICAL
CONSIDERATIONS

IS IT JUST A TEST OR IS A TRANSITION COMING?

NOW THAT A FEW things are established concerning pastoral transition, I want to get personal and discuss some nitty-gritty details. I heard recently of a pastor who resigned his position after only a few months of pastoring, citing personal issues and problems within the church that he couldn't change.

Ministry can be difficult at times, especially, when too many of the wrong voices are speaking into the minister's life and when someone's level of experience, knowledge, and anointing doesn't match well with the challenges presented and responsibilities required. Confusion is the only possible result, which isn't God's will, as Paul declared in 1 Corinthians 14:33, *"For God is not the author of confusion, but of peace..."*

How many times have you been listening to a song or a speaker on the radio and been annoyed by that sudden blaring, "this is a test" tone? Even more obnoxious is the follow-up explanation. You get it, right? If it had been real, then the emergency broadcast system wouldn't have been annoying. But in this case, it was just a test, just a precaution, in case of a future sudden change of normality, and it interrupted what you'd been focused on.

In my own experiences of upcoming change, I've felt unusual feelings of restlessness in my life. Those out-of-the-ordinary thoughts, emotions, and agitations just seem to appear out of the blue. I've learned that those things are indicators of something other than what they seem to be, on the surface.

But, before jumping to conclusions that a radical change is on the horizon, I ask myself if this is only a test. If it's a test, then jumping ship isn't an option. I have seen, firsthand, what happens when a minister bails on his purpose when, instead, he should have stood "...still and see the salvation of the Lord." The results of wrong decisions are spiritually horrifying.

The most important first step, once you've wrapped your brain around what the uneasiness means, is to figure out if God is prompting you to leave the current situation and to start over somewhere else or to stay and lead differently. Either way you must immediately realize that it's a season of new personal growth.

And, of course, this is a time for you to reach out to your close ministerial mentors to get their insight. I hope you have someone in your life like that, someone who has veto power over the decisions in your life. It might be your spouse, a pastor, close friend or district official. And if there's no one in your life with veto power, I strongly suggest you find that person and develop a mentoring relationship with them.

At one point in our lives, Lisa and I were both completely confident that a major change was coming in our ministry. This transition would have taken us away from a pastoral assignment we been working in for three years. But, before we made the final decision to resign, I called a pastor who had often spoken into our lives. After sharing our thoughts, feelings, confirmations, and certainties with him, he simply said that, no, it wasn't the right time. Hearing that was difficult, but we followed that pastor's wise direction, and God honored our obedience by blessing us with an additional seven years of favor there.

Allowing someone oversight in your life is a safe place to live. Their investment will bring clarity to your decisions and will help cut through the confusion. Then, when the time is right, things will fall into place the way they're supposed to, and that elusive confirmation will come.

IS IT TIME TO RESIGN?

MORE THAN TWENTY-FIVE YEARS AGO, I heard the powerful and passionate Vesta Mangun speak at a national conference in Alexandria, Louisiana about fulfilling one's personal ordination. Her session literally changed my life. That day, I accepted the truth that my ordination from Heaven is not yours and the ordination you are responsible for is not mine. No two are exactly the same. I haven't forgotten what took place in my mind and heart in that service. As a result, I live every day working to wholeheartedly fulfill what God desires out of my life. That's my responsibility.

Accomplishing this lifelong, all-consuming task, requires staying open and fluid to divine direction. The apostle Paul said it best in 1 Corinthians 6:19-20: *"What? know ye not that your body is the temple of the Holy Ghost which is in you, which ye have of God, and ye are not your own? For ye are bought with a price: therefore glorify God in your body, and in your spirit, which are God's."*

Internalizing this happens by first believing every minister must be true to himself and the unique calling he possesses, including moving on when God directs. If this really is a transition ordained by God, then minister has to own this new reality and be good with it. From personal experience, "being good with it" feels impossible at times, but he needs to work on his attitudes until he is.

Once the minister has settled God's calling in his mind, he needs to communicate that calling with his wife, giving her adequate time to process and take ownership of the coming transition.

Third, they need to work together as a unified front to clearly share the decision with their children about the future direction for their family.

Finally, it's time to share the plan with the congregation, and it's important to be honest, open and transparent. They need to hear messages of assurance like this:

"This is my specific calling. (Detail your past, present, and purposeful future.) God brought me from somewhere or something else to this place, and this is what He did while we served in this capacity. In order to stay in the will of God, like I have taught and expected of you, I have to hold myself, and my family to the same standard. God is directing us to another ministry focus, but be assured, if God is leading us to another place, He is also calling someone else to this responsibility. Just because we are departing, doesn't in any way mean you'll be left without a voice or a shepherd. God has prepared someone to take this church to the next dimension."

It's so important to communicate the upcoming transition in the right way, otherwise the people become fearful, and will begin to entertain tormenting thoughts, thinking that, when the pastor leaves, that things will automatically turn out badly.

In many cases (hopefully, in most cases), it should get better. Transition, done right, is not a negative thing; it's positive. The church can look forward to reaching a new level the former pastor was not ordained or anointed to lead them to. When God spoke to Moses, remember it was clearly revealed, Joshua would, *"go over before this people, and he shall cause them to inherit the land which thou shalt see."*

Resignation shouldn't be an off-the-cuff decision or knee-jerk reaction to frustration or difficulty. Instead, strive to help people understand the larger picture and the purpose of God concerning the local church and its leaders.

Strategically and prayerfully consider—and plan for—each of these questions so that concerns will be minimized for the minister, his family and the congregation:

- When do I resign?
- How long do I stay after resigning?
- Do I help in the process of choosing the next pastor or leave it to others?

Early in my ministry I decided not to look back with regrets but to consistently serve, to the best of my abilities, wherever God has me. Then, when God pushes me towards a new ministerial transition, I don't feel remorse about how I operated while serving, what I actually accomplished, or how I left.

It's those who refuse to walk this challenging road of ministerial transition that fall short of what Heaven attended for their own lives, and for the advancement of the kingdom.

By the way, if you find yourself as a part of a congregation that's experiencing a ministerial transition, seek advice from active leaders and fellow saints who have experienced a pastoral change. Their help can play a major role in your growth, understanding, and spiritual maturity.

Later, I will share about three men who spoke into my father-in-law's life during a critical time of transition. What they each contributed cannot even be quantified four decades later. Outside investment is often the key to making it through the challenges of that time and it will add immensely to your ability to flourish in transitional seasons.

MINISTERIAL RETIREMENT: EMBRACING THE UNKNOWN

AN UNKNOWN FUTURE or even worse, the thought of no future at all, is debilitating for anyone, but even more so, for people who have given their lives in ministry. What's next for them, when they transition out of full time, active ministry? This is one of the greatest fears that ministers grapple with.

It isn't out of the ordinary for people in the midst of change to feel uncertain and apprehensive about tomorrow. They wonder what it is going to look like. They ask, "How will my life be different? Will the new reality be something I can handle?"

Many years ago, I was in San Antonio, Texas riding in a car with two of my closest ministry friends. We were laughing, talking, and enjoying some down time together, when, in a split second, everything changed.

Immediately in front of us, on the busy interstate, a vehicle began to flip, end-over-end. When the mayhem stopped, the out-of-control car was upside-down, in the middle of the median, and we happen to be the closest bystanders to the wreck. It was so real and life-altering, that, as I share this event, I can see, hear, smell, and feel everything transpiring again.

We jumped out and ran to the scene, finding a man hanging upside-down, strapped in by the seatbelt. He was semiconscious and completely oblivious to what had just happened. At first glance, he looked okay, but, as you know, things are not always as they appear. Both of my friends reached in the vehicle, gently touched the man, and began asking him questions. He didn't respond verbally, and suddenly a stream of blood started pouring from the top of his head. Imagine what it felt like, kneeling in the hot Texas heat, under a demolished car, trying to keep a severely-injured person from moving. We applied pressure to the gaping wound, wondered what else was damaged, and impatiently waited for the paramedics to arrive. All of the bystanders were literally holding the life of this stranger in their hands. It was a brief ordeal —maybe a half hour or so—and once the professionals made it to the scene, we were able to leave the situation in their hands.

Now imagine living in that environment of heightened awareness day-after-day, night-after-night, for decades! The only difference is that you, now, are responsible for not just that individual, but many other individuals' souls. The continual weight of where each will spend eternity is almost unbearable and incomprehensible. Welcome to the ministry.

It's real, but just as medical professionals respond over and over again, doing their work with precision and excellence, so do those in ministry. Something interesting happens over time. No matter how heavy the pressure or load is, you learn to love, welcome, and shoulder the responsibility.

Now, think about what it would feel like, for that life of serving to be, done, over, vamoose, gone. Some say they would welcome it, and that might be the case, but, for many, that drastic change of pace and responsibility is more than they want to adjust to.

For a long time, three times a week you find yourself in a pulpit, providing life-giving words. Other days and nights are filled with meeting after meeting, encounter after encounter, resuscitating a marriage, provided antidotes to life for a young person, comforting a family facing loss and being the spiritual advisor to those who are in your care. Then, suddenly, those responsibilities are gone. You can see how you'd struggle with identity and purpose. Because of this fear, some pastors hold on too long.

Sadly, finding significance outside of the pastoral role is virtually impossible for some. It's the only life they know. It's the only life they are willing to live. Because of this, both the minister and the church member suffer unnecessary pain.

So, here's a big question: Retirement. Do ministers ever really retire?

Truthfully, I've observed that retirement isn't easy for ministers! A person's self-worth can be greatly affected and often severely tested after their years of pastoral investment. It's hard to feel comforted by the return on efforts when they're no longer able to contribute. But here's the hard question, the one that reveals the bottom line truth: Is the minister kingdom-minded or in self-preservation mode? Is the church helped or hindered by his continued leadership?

Unfortunately, exit strategies are not abundant in the scripture. Oh, how many former pastors wish they were! The Bible doesn't offer a collection of stories about calling it quits.

My friend, Pastor Jonathan Barley, alluded to one reason we don't have a specific biblically spelled-out guide for pastoral transition. The truth is, the most common way New Testament church leaders ended their ministries was death by martyrdom, long before the thoughts of retirement ever entered the realm of possibility. Obviously, times have changed.

RETIRE—THEN "UN-RETIRE?"

SOMETIMES, an older or previous long-term pastor retires, but after stepping aside and someone new fills the pastoral position, the now-retired pastor has a change-of-heart about no longer being the decision-maker and primary leader. There could be different reasons for that:

- The former pastor feels the loss of identity, or of purpose, or, even of finances.
- Revival starts to occur under the new pastor's leadership —a revival the retired pastor believed for, pressed for, and prayed for, but didn't happened during his time of leading. Seeing prayers answered and the work rewarded has the potential to rejuvenate the retired pastor and cause him to think and feel like he can step back into the former role.
- The church experiences decline, and the retired pastor is concerned that what he worked for is going to be lost.
- After a time of retirement, the former pastor feels rested

and begins to see things differently, once out from under
the pressure.

- He's being ignored or underappreciated in his new role
  and isn't being cared for, or is overlooked or even
  forgotten.

I've seen this (or similar) scenarios happening often in pastoral
transitions. What happens when he steps back in? In many cases,
the result is a loss of trajectory for everyone involved, including the
church, the former leader, and the present pastor. Everyone and
everything suffers.

The only way for the new leader to get around all those concerns is
to continue to honor the retired pastor and show sincere
appreciation for all he built. Determine to recognize and credit past
efforts, no matter their size or effectiveness. The reality is, someone
provided a foundation of possibility for the incoming leader to work
with and build upon.

Take it from someone who has started over with nothing several
times. No matter what you think or feel, having some people, some
contacts, and some assets is much better than starting with nothing.
I implore you to appreciate whatever you have to work with and
show that appreciation every chance you can.

WHAT'S THE ROLE OF THE NEW PASTOR?

ON THE FLIP side of this transition, is the role of the new pastor and how he's often hindered in his efforts towards the betterment of the church. So many times, he's not given the liberty to move forward because he's being controlled by the former leader's expectations, or by the people's jaded, concrete, or limited opinions. In these types of cases, it's a real struggle for him to maintain a positive mental state.

So, what should the new leader do? Back off and establish an unwavering confidence in God to orchestrate the situation. In the end, it's the Lord's church and He knows where He wants to take that congregation in the future.

WHAT ABOUT THE CHURCH MEMBERS?

THEN, there are the church members. Many are fearful about what will change with the new leadership. Will they still feel like the church is *their* church? Or will it change so much that they no longer feel comfortable there? Optimistically, they stand to benefit, even if they're unsure about how the transition will ultimately go. The new pastor might relate, in an even greater way, to where they are as individuals, and can minister to them more beneficially, than the former leader did.

At the same time, it's important to acknowledge that they can experience loss, if they let hurt, bitterness, and strife into their heart. This most naturally happens when they didn't realize the transition was coming and immediately develop a bad attitude toward it. The wrong attitude could potentially cause them to lose ground spiritually, which could negatively affect their future.

DON'T FORGET TO REMEMBER THE PASTOR'S FAMILY

LAST, but certainly not least, the minister's family, both his children and his wife, are also greatly affected by a transition, especially if they happen often. Coming and going diminishes a children's opportunities to feel settled because they are uncertain of their parent's long-term plan or goal of the ministry.

The minister's wife may find the transition to be the most difficult of all, because personal connections tend to be extremely important to her. It can be hard for her to continually be thrust into the middle of a new crowd of people, working to find her way into the lives of new people and in a new location. Or when it's a case of retirement, they have to find a new life altogether.

The reason, more times than not, that those in ministry are hesitant to take action is they really don't want to face those unknown, yet, unavoidable challenges. I'm convinced that, if more individuals were confident that everything would end up right, and they believed they could get through the ministerial transition with no regrets, we would hear more testimonies of bold steps. But it's not easy getting to that type of faith.

WHO GETS A VOICE IN THE TRANSITION?

ONE THING that makes a pastoral transition extremely hard is when too many difficult personalities get involved. Many times, there are controlling individuals, influential families, someone who's disgruntled, or someone who wants to be recognized as a power player in the transition. When those people give their unsolicited opinions, chaos often occurs. If you have experienced a negative ministry change in the past, most likely, the cause stemmed from one or more of these contributors.

These types of issues should not be part of a pastoral transition but, sadly, they happen in some situations. People like to be in control. Most often, those power players are individuals with wealth, membership longevity, or complete disengagement under normal circumstances, and they see a transition time as a good option for trying to push their manipulative agendas.

These transitions have spiritual connotations and consequences and, even more so, kingdom importance, so it's vital that those involved have the right attitude.

When control is the name of the game, jealousy can rise up with people demanding to be heard and, at the very least, considered. Leaders feel threatened. Otherwise good folks experience feelings of hurt, especially if they weren't included in the talks early-on or were oblivious to the inside scoop and they didn't know, in advance, that the transition was coming.

Those types of stressors can sideline everything. It is important for those feeling marginalized to be reminded that the new person coming in would not have the opportunity to guide the church if it wasn't for the former leader extending the official invite to consider the pastorate. In most cases, a destructive coup is not what you are dealing with, so work to explain the situation, resolve it, and then move in the direction of divine expectation.

Often, there is an undue amount of personal positioning on the part of both the ministry and the congregation, with select people trying to get what they want, and ministers making decisions based on what's going to potentially most benefit themselves. In those cases, everyone needs to be reminded that this is kingdom business; it's not about the individuals.

An additional group that comes to mind that can be an issue are the outside voices. It's imperative to be certain that everyone who is speaking into the situation are voices who have a heart, first, for the people, next, for the continued effectiveness of the church in the community, and then, for the ministers involved. Be careful not to have too many voices offering their thoughts. God is not the author of confusion.

Not just anyone should have access to your life or your church transitional situation. I remember some unsolicited phone calls I received during a pastoral change. If I had listened to the advice I'd received, it would have completely decimated the exact plan God had for us during that time. Churches are destroyed, ministers misaligned, and congregations are scattered at times, because of too many voices giving the wrong advice.

When outside family and friends are trying to influence spiritual decisions, many times, important factors like successful prior experience, training, qualifications, calling and purpose are not even considered. What a devastating mistake! And that mistake can have negative eternal results, not to mention all the tragedy, hurt, confusion, delay of the harvest, and fearful stories that invariably surface in connection with the transition.

So much valuable time is wasted when we fall into the trap of thinking that it's all about us, the minister. It's not. It's about God's plan, His people, and His church—all of which are completely and solely His! Remember He said, *"for I the Lord thy God am a jealous God."* Exodus 20:5

We need to be careful not to find ourselves at fault for allowing outsiders to have unnecessary control, pulling strings, trying to impose their will and desire in order to influence the process. While they believe their input will help the transition, often, it doesn't, because their heart is not in the right place.

Actually, it's most important to get input from those who are responsible for the present stability and future potential of the church, including its pastors, board members, district officials, and/or a council of elders. What would be best would be to have input from all of those people, but, of course, it really depends on how the church is set up, legally.

Once decisions are made, and everyone is settled, be aware that sometimes, the new pastor becomes the target of unresolved difficulties with past leadership and finds himself tasked with handling someone else's issues. Expect it; some people will test the new authority to see where the boundaries are. It's important for both the pastor and the church member to understand this and not be surprised.

I've also found some things that weren't a problem or issue for the previous administration will surface in the presence of a new pastor. One way to move through those challenging seasons is to place everyone on the same page, at the same level, and with the same expectations. Don't take anyone or anything for granted.

This is accomplished through clear, revealing conversations, providing assurance one-on-one to as many individuals as possible and answering questions in a general sense from the pulpit.

But, it's not one-sided and it works both ways. The exiting leader can come under uninitiated scrutiny and accusation, which has the potential to hang-on for days, months, and years. The ongoing strength of a congregation can quickly be jeopardized if this isn't immediately quelled.

Work to always make the greatest influence in the church to be the single voice coming from behind the pulpit. And if you happen to be that voice, listen only to the spiritual voices you've made room for in your life. My recommendation is if you are surrendering to their counsel, make certain that they are people who have nothing to gain or lose as a result of the transition.

IV

LEARNING FROM OTHERS' TRANSITION EXPERIENCES

BEEN THERE, DONE THAT
—R.L. MITCHELL, SR

AN OLD SCOTTISH proverb says that "Confession is good for the soul." No, it's not a Bible verse, like many would lead us to believe, although, there are many scriptures readily found bearing out the principle.

Ready or not, right or wrong, here's a confession for you. I don't ever remember a time when ministry and ministry transition wasn't a real everyday part of my life. It feels like I grew up and started ministry right in the middle of transition times.

Recently, I heard a guest on *The Portfolio Life* podcast with Jeff Goins address a similar reality. He shared that how we're raised has a huge effect on what we are familiar with later on in life. For me, from a child, I was raised around ministry, so souls, church work, and ministering to people are all I've really ever known.

My initial perspective of pastoral changes came and was developed as a member of a pastor's family. Growing up in a minister's home provides a unique environment for transitional insight. In those early days, I observed it all as the son of a minister, but not as the minister himself.

My dad, Robert Mitchell, Sr., moved our family to Dayton, Ohio from Houston, Texas when I was four years old to become the pastor of The Apostolic Lighthouse, a numerically small church. Over the next five years, until I was nine, I watched the church grow into a congregation of several hundred people.

From my childish point of view, it was sixty months, give or take a few, of effectiveness, evidenced by numerical and financial advancement along with added assets of both land and buildings. To me, at that time, I sincerely believed the way things happened there in Ohio, under my father's leadership, was the way it should be done everywhere, and the same types of things would happen just like that, in every situation.

Reminiscing, I have many fond memories and friendships from those formative years we spent in the Buckeye state, and thankfully several of those friendships, established at such a young age, remain to this day.

After we transitioned to the next place, my parents weren't ever invited back to visit nor were they consulted about anything at that particular church again. As a side note, I did visit years later after starting to preach, but wasn't readily welcomed. The leadership treated me reluctantly and distantly, but the people, who knew me as a child, embraced me and were kind.

My observation and experience says that once a minister moves on, there isn't much appreciation given, unless the succeeding minister is kingdom-minded and has the wherewithal to understand that, "If I have seen further, it is by standing on the shoulders of giants." (Isaac Newton) I hope to never forget that it's as much about those who have gone before us, laying the groundwork and investing untold hours of effort than what is currently occurring though us.

By doing this, the fulfillment of Paul's instruction to the Romans takes place, *"Render therefore to all their dues: tribute to whom tribute is due; custom to whom custom; fear to whom fear; honour to whom honour."* Romans 13:7

I've found in my own life that a person will never go wrong showing respect and honor to people for their investment and time, and it really doesn't matter if the contribution considered was great or small in your eyes.

Before moving on, let me share that, close to thirty years later, I went back to the church of my childhood. This time it was via an invitation to preach and the leadership was completely different.

As God would have it, the present pastoral family was directly connected to the first convert my parents won to the Lord in 1969. The story was completely different the second time around and I might note, they blessed us greatly.

My father's second pastorate took us back to our home, the Lone Star State, and he became the pastor of Stonewall Pentecostal Church in Houston, Texas. It was comparable in number to the previous church in Dayton, but in this case, it seemed to be a greater responsibility, because he was assuming someone else's successful work and a notable and well-known congregation.

Great things happened for him over the years at this new church, including membership growth and again, an increase of land and facilities. My father continued for eighteen years in his Houston pastorate and I was able to continue observing from the perspective of the pastor's home. This exposure transpired up-close for the first decade, until I moved away in my second year college.

During this time of living in another state, the church, from a distance, appeared to rebound from every storm that came along— of which there were many, as I recall. I mentioned in my first book, *Transition: Life's Unavoidable Reality, A Guide to Successfully*

Navigating Change, (www.robertmitchell2.com), that church life in Houston, Texas was the big leagues. It was different on every level, but my father accomplished much, while treading in deep waters. As a result, I saw and was conditioned to expect transition to be positive.

Having more understanding now and being removed from both situations for almost three decades, the two churches my late father pastored were quite different in many ways. In the first location, he was limited financially, was a novice pastor having only been in ministry a few short years, the culture of the people in the north was different than his Louisiana upbringing and the entire responsibility to lead was resting on his shoulders alone. Previously, he had worked under another pastor. When he transitioned to the next place of ministry, he was forced to let go of yesterday and deal with several new issues: quick growth, insurrection from the pew, people leaving the church, unethical neighboring pastors, and the congregation's main connection to a previous long-term leader.

But remember, I was viewing it from the place of being a member of the pastor's family, and I didn't know all the details of things going on behind the scenes. From what I could tell, it seemed there was commendable success in both locations.

It's interesting how perspectives change based on awareness and information.

What I saw, and subsequently learned from my own father's pastoral experience was valuable. The first church he pastored lacked strength when pastoral transition came. That church was made up of a large percentage of new Christians, who were not prepared to stand on their own after his rather brief, five-year pastoral tenure there.

I experienced the same thing personally, it when I seriously considered the reality of leaving our first pastorate in Asheville after two short years. Looking back, I know that there's no way the young congregation would have survived had Lisa and I left that early in the process. The settling and establishment of a secure foundation had yet to develop. The church, like my father's church in Dayton, would have declined, struggled, and most likely suffered loss.

From my dad's experience and my own observation of similar transitional times, after we left, the people were smothered by a different type of leader, one who apparently felt threatened by what had been previously accomplished and didn't understand the need of the moment.

To continue building on an already-laid foundation demands being crystal clear on the history, current state, and future journey of the church and its congregants. A major shift in direction and purpose doesn't have to occur with every leadership change. It's an honorable thing to be the succeeding leader but it's so important to learn as much as possible so you won't be so disadvantaged, coming from outside the church.

UNCERTAINTY IS THE ONLY CERTAINTY—R.L. MITCHELL, JR.

SERVING in the position of actually leading and being responsible for the direction and spiritual survival of a congregation was much different than just watching as my parents led. The responsibility ultimately found its way onto my shoulders, and it was definitely eye-opening, on-the-job learning!

Early Pastoring

I look back at my first attempt in leading in a pastoral role and I know it was premature. I was not prepared for the magnitude of that responsibility. The situation happened out of necessity more than a true calling and it was a difficult environment with an unhealthy and unhappy culture. Plus, I was young.

I didn't realize that there is a huge difference between standing behind a pulpit to deliver a message and actually pastoring people with situations that a one time, inspirational sermon is not going to fix.

My wife, Lisa, and I were newly married, and she was even

younger than me. Without having a clue of what to do, we were thrust into a challenging circumstance and environment, possessing no real connection with the church. People were confused, and, at the same time, were being influenced by a lay-leader who proved to be a "wolf in sheep's clothing." This individual was working behind our backs to bring destruction and to gain control. Ironically, this person had ongoing hidden issues in their own life.

An important directive found in the gospel of Matthew: *"Beware of false prophets, which come to you in sheep's clothing, but inwardly they are ravening wolves."* Matthew 7:15

The apostle Paul in 1 Thessalonians 5:12 gave this additional warning and portion of pastoral instruction: *"And we beseech you, brethren, to know them which labour among you, and are over you in the Lord, and admonish you."*

Oh, the value of those words and the weight they carry, as I painfully recall those inaugural days of pastoring. I should point out my sole responsibility was the pulpit; everything else was being carried out by others on the ministerial team. It was a year of struggle on every front, except in the area of sermonizing, and honestly, it almost cost us our marriage, our sanity, and our fledgling ministry, all of which were new, fragile, and vulnerable.

Without question, we were intensely tested. That is the "kind" way of describing those difficult times. But everyone in ministry, like it or not, will be tested at some point. Oh, that there were more transparent, open, clear, and direct ministerial mentors willing to help others realize their calling and place.

Evangelist

Before that first try at pastoral leadership, I had evangelized for ten years, which was a win, on every front, and on every level. It was also a constant eye-opening experience and I realized after a decade that it wasn't supposed to last forever. It was simply a ten-year training ground.

As an evangelist, you're in different cities, different states, different countries, different cultures, different environments, different homes, and different hotels. You deal with a vast amount of good and bad restaurants, laundromats, cleaners, personalities, and even climates that are different. Time zones are different, and you are forced to eat and sleep on different schedules. Churches are different, worship styles are different, leadership is different, expectations are different, demands are different, people have different beliefs, and different standards of living and income amounts are different. Everything was constantly changing.

We were forced to learn constantly since everything continually changed. We were in a different place every few days, for all those years, with all the uncertainties that came along with it. Because we learned to adjust, and actually be comfortable with that constant state of flux, we thought we were ready for pastoring, but we found out differently in that brief one-year stint.

Church Planter

The next major step for us was in the completely different avenue of church planting.

In March 1997, Lisa and I moved to the spiritually-challenged picturesque city of Asheville, North Carolina. This relocation developed into ten years of in-the-trenches ministry. During this season, church-planting truly became a life's work for us— something we had never previously dreamt of.

Had we listened to the negative talk about what a "big step of faith" we were taking in starting churches, there would be no testimony of His goodness. Critics even thought we'd never achieve our personal desires or enjoy a recognized ministry. What they didn't understand was that acquiring earthly things meant little to us when compared to eternal treasures gained through obedience. Some people even had the audacity to suggest our planting actions were a sure death sentence. They didn't know how we were going to make it. If you're hearing similar things, refuse to entertain those detractors.

We heard things like, "It's hard, lonely, difficult, and impossible to build a church in this city." "Current generations and the climate of the times do not lend themselves to evangelism." "People don't want truth or to be told what to do." "No commitment is to be found in this hour." Those statements, along with many others, sounding much the same, could have derailed our willingness to walk in surrender to a higher purpose.

If you listen to dissenting voices, instead of His, you'll find yourself stressing over hypothetical happenings, what ifs, and the inaccurate perspectives of fear-filled individuals. It's the frivolous opinions of others and the trivial matters of the moment that are most often responsible for the inactivity of spiritual people. If you're called, count on it, God will provide!

Live subject to God's opinion, not the naysayers. Matthew 10:28 declares, *"And fear not them which kill the body, but are not able to kill the soul: but rather fear him which is able to destroy both soul and body in hell."* Don't worry about the things you can't change. Instead, focus more on what you can contribute.

Out of that very willingness—along with extreme effort—The Church of Pentecost was established. The back story is that we had been exposed to church planting through the frontline attempts of family, friends, and acquaintances. From direct observation and financial investment, the possibility of home missions was birthed within us.

We stayed there for a decade. Then, we experienced an

unexpected move to Fayetteville, North Carolina to pastor the well-established First United Pentecostal Church.

I don't make that move thinking it was our life's work, but it was, without question, a divine assignment. That new direction came out of the blue, and it was necessitated by the former pastor's retirement and subsequent request for me to become the next pastor.

Pastor Jesse Williams shared with me a few years before he passed away, how God had specifically directed him, by speaking to him during a time of prayer, that Lisa and I should succeed him. Pastor Williams went as far as pointing out the place in a prayer room where he heard from God. It most assuredly was Heaven-ordained. The many divine happenings that transpired over the following four years, under our leadership in Fayetteville, were the evidence.

Some of the experiences we had as evangelists helped us succeed during the time of church planting and then all those combined experiences helped us when we moved on to assume the pastorate of the dynamic First Church, with its long, rich history.

I would be remiss not to briefly mention the history at play. First Church Fayetteville was six months away from celebrating a forty-year anniversary when we were elected to the senior pastor position. The church had been started in the living room of the former pastor and his family of six. Within seven short years, the church was averaging around seven hundred in Sunday morning attendance and even experienced a high-water mark Easter attendance of over 1000 people within ten years of its inception.

To me this was almost hard to fathom, but once I wrapped my head around what was actually in the foundation of that church, I had my primary marching orders. I needed to simply tap into what the church was established on, and focus on a revival of the supernatural, apostolic truth, lost souls, community impact, and uncommon growth.

But the transition wasn't without difficulties. In one instance, my wife had a conversation with a young woman who felt blindsided by our transition into this church and was suddenly facing our different style and type of leadership.

This lady boldly told Lisa, "We don't like you and don't even know why you're here."

My wife responded, "Have you ever thought about where we came from? Have you thought about how the people in our previous location felt toward us like you feel toward the former pastor here? They loved us and didn't want us to leave them. Have you even considered this works both ways? You say you don't like us, and honestly, we're not sure how we feel about you either."

As a new pastor, don't forget they know the former pastor, and his disposition, but they're not sure about you as the next leader, and honestly, they really don't care about you yet. They're still trying to come to terms with the "news" of departure.

This is a two-way street; it's not just good for the leader, and bad for the saint, or good for the saint and bad for the leader. Everyone involved must work together and do their collective best to get through transitional season, even with all its challenges, misunderstandings, and ups and downs.

By the way, the person my wife had the difficult conversation with ended up being one of our greatest supporters. She said to Lisa, "I had never considered your feelings before. I'm going to give you a chance." And it ended up working out fine.

With that being said, the story immediately comes to mind of how hard it was for us to leave The Church of Pentecost, the first church we started in North Carolina. I know now, in order arrive at the next place God was leading us to, we had to unwillingly leave the place we were comfortable in and connected to.

For us, this church was our baby, like the experiences first time parents have in the process of pregnancy, delivery, and successful childrearing. It was something we birthed without realizing we really could accomplish such a monumental task. We understood and related well to the people who made up the congregation. Each person was dear to us. We had worked so hard and long to build and establish that church and, in our flesh, we would rather have stayed forever.

Of course, I didn't look or feel like this in the beginning. Some organizational, religious, and well-meaning onlookers called that particular area "a burned-over field." They said it was a graveyard for preachers because of the many previous, unsuccessful attempts to start a Spirit-filled, apostolic church in the city. From all indicators and reports we were hearing, Western North Carolina wasn't an easy place to attempt church planting, but the resolve and mindset we possessed was, *"...With men it is impossible, but not with God: for with God all things are possible."* Mark 10:27

It started out with us feeling a bit like those two lone men, Joshua and Caleb, in the presence of the other spies. They were outnumbered by detractors but were motivated by faith in a miracle-working God. *"And Caleb stilled the people before Moses, and said, Let us go up at once, and possess it; for we are well able to overcome it."* Numbers 13:30

For the most part, we went from an ideal life on the road as evangelists, where you receive a lot of attention, to starting a church, where, not only is there no particular recognition, but you're handed nothing, and expected to do something with it.

As an evangelist, you see immediate results. There's a full calendar ahead of you. Most of the spiritual impact that results from preaching revivals was actually previously prepared before we even pulled into town, and for the next few services, weeks, or months, things were good. The impact was ready-made, really.

It was so different as a church planter and one meaningful breakthrough came for me when I stopped desiring to go out and evangelize again. Instead, everything was stripped away. I was given a city, nothing more, nothing less, and I had to step up and do something with it or drown in the process. Once again, it was God, propelling us out of our comfort zone.

Planting that church took years of sacrifice, labor, consistency, and constantly operating with determined intention. All that work and sensitivity was worth it, because something lasting came out of it in the form of the kingdom extension, and an established church.

People were converted, the assets of a building and land were gathered, and money was left in the bank to clear all debts, including the mortgage, when we ultimately resigned that pastorate. There was a healthy culture of progress within the church family, committed leaders and an exceptional ministry team. The church had a spiritual environment lending itself toward continued growth and two decades later, the church is still going strong, for which, we are thankful.

What a transition that was, to go from a decade of successful evangelizing, which included preaching in an average of two hundred and twenty-five revival services a year, to launching a church with little to no resources, in a difficult area of the country, and actually accomplishing something enduring for God there. Harry S. Truman said, "It is amazing what you can accomplish if you do not care who gets the credit."

We were ill-equipped in many areas, but we were willing, organized, and possessed a passion for personal evangelism. Even the Children of Israel found themselves comfortable in various locations on their way to the Promise Land. In Deuteronomy 1:6-8, 2:2-3, God was forced to tell them when it was time to move.

"The Lord our God spake unto us in Horeb, saying, Ye have dwelt long enough in this mount: Turn you, and take your journey, and go to the mount of the Amorites, and unto all the places nigh thereunto, in the plain, in the hills, and in the vale, and in the south, and by the sea side, to the land of the Canaanites, and unto Lebanon, unto the great river, the river Euphrates. Behold, I have set the land before you: go in and possess the land which the Lord sware unto your fathers, Abraham, Isaac, and Jacob, to give unto them and to their seed after them."

"And the Lord spake unto me, saying, Ye have compassed this mountain long enough: turn you northward."

When I look back and evaluate the transition in Asheville to the next pastor, I can see it went well. We were intentional in how we opened the door for him, introduced him, promoted him, and deferred questions to him in the church. This may sound extreme, but through our influence, we required the congregation to honor and respect him in an authentic way, giving him the time and opportunity to settle in to the new environment as his first pastorate. We worked to support his efforts and not to work against them.

Because I knew a transition was coming, I worked strategically for several months, both from the pulpit and in personal interactions, to prepare the church so they wouldn't be caught off guard. I spoke about the individual connection people have with God, and with the truth. I reminded them about Who it was who had changed their lives and that knowing Him was more important than knowing anyone else. Their connection was not just with my leadership style or me. It was with God. It was with the truth. It was about their experience in Him.

In a sense this was about creating space and distance from fleshly ties and promoting a need for more intimate connection with Majesty. In order to accomplish this, the interactions with us personally had to become less frequent. I knew we had laid a strong foundation, and the people not only heard, but also responded to the message. As a result, there was no significant numerical loss during the transition. From all outside appearance, things remained close to the same in structure, involvement, and faithfulness. This was an indication of spiritual maturity on the congregation's part.

Because they were more connected to the Lord than to my wife and me, people stayed through the pastoral transition. It was difficult to leave, but extremely rewarding for us when folks held on when less spiritually mature people might have gotten lost in the shuffle.

THE SAFETY OF EXPERIENCED COUNSEL—JOHNNY GODAIR

DURING TIMES OF CHANGE, both ministers and churches need mentors, peers, and voices of wisdom more than any other thing—including special tools, training, or equipment. Confidants will provide ideas, thoughts, perspectives, experience, and reason.

I'm sure you've realized by now that experience has been a great teacher in my life through all the ministerial transitions. It is said, "Experience is the teacher of all things." The infamous Roman leader Julius Caesar recorded the earliest known version of this proverb, in 'De Bello Civili' (c. 52 B.C.). Others have added to the statement by describing the teacher as the "greatest." Without question, there are lessons to learn at the hands of experience, but one must be willing to either do the work to unearth those lessons or have others make them plain and palatable.

When you don't have the experience, then it's important to look for the expertise of others who've successfully walked through transitions and have those voices speak into your life. My father-in-law, Johnny Godair, experienced that. He's a man of practical, effective wisdom, which is a rare quality not many in ministry are exposed to today. Here's how he got to where he is now:

After evangelizing for a few years as a late teen, he started a church in the small town of Malden, Missouri when he was in his early twenties. Under his leadership, the congregation grew from zero to an average of 300 Sunday attenders, in ten years. During his first three years at that church, he saw no growth, which caused many family members and friends to tell him he should go back to evangelizing. However, he stayed with it, despite the doubts the others had about it, because he felt a call and directive from the Lord.

What I learned from him when he shared this experience, was that not everyone will understand my spiritual path. As an individual minister I am required by God to walk it out, be obedient, and fulfill my personal ordination. (There's the word ordination again) It's my unique divinely-designed destiny.

When he began to feel that a time of change was coming from that successful pastorate, he connected with three different men, who each contributed to his noteworthy transition. These three men were serving in national roles of leadership within the United Pentecostal Church, but they took time to give direction and encouragement to a young local pastor.

First, he set up a meeting with Rev. J.T. Pugh, the acting Home Missions Division Director to ask how to leave, how to resign, and how to work through the process. Pastor Pugh gave my father-in-law practical, nuts-and-bolts advice about how to transition successfully.

He suggested ways to resign, how to prepare the people, what he needed to be aware of when it came to the legalities, and how to consider the congregation's well-being through it all. Those few things are so important.

More on this later, but when the legal aspects of pastoral transition is considered, it shows proper stewardship to both God and man. Jesus said, in Luke 20:25, *"And he said unto them, Render therefore unto Caesar the things which be Caesar's, and unto God the things which be God's."*

The Kingdom of God and the world around are done a tremendous disservice when the business of the church is handled in a roughshod, careless manner! I would be remiss not to mention the testimony of Jacob. The scripture says, *"And he said, Thy name shall be called no more Jacob, but Israel: for as a prince hast thou power with God and with men, and hast prevailed."* Genesis 32:28

Being in favor with God and man is an honorable thing. Some people obtain spiritual approval but fail miserably in their effort for natural excellence and vice versa. Prevailing in both areas should be the intention. Let me stretch this to say poor professional dealings cast a negative light on the church and its ministries, in the community. Ask those who have experienced it. In some instances, it becomes virtually impossible to ever recover from.

The second man to help my father-in-law's transition was Rev. J.R. Ensey. He was serving as the Secretary of the Home Missions Division, and he talked to my father-in-law about his potential next location, since, after resigning from the church, he would need somewhere to go to continue his ministry. Other friends and acquaintances had spoken to him about the possibility of starting a church in the Dakotas, but it was J.R. Ensey who talked to him about the East Coast and pointed him specifically towards North Carolina.

The third man was the Promotional Director of the same organizational division, Rev. V. A. Guidroz. When my father-in-law moved to North Carolina, he assumed he'd need to work at a secular job to support his family financially, while he also worked to establish the new church. Instead, and by the Lord's design, V.A.

Guidroz started opening doors for him to be the guest speaker at various revival conferences and growth events around the country. Honorariums from those short-term speaking opportunities made it possible for him to put more of his focus on planting the church and, even though he didn't have a congregation initially, my father-in-law never had to find that secular job. In April 2019, he celebrated his forty-sixth pastoral anniversary at First Pentecostal Church, in Durham, North Carolina.

Three specific men spoke into my father-in-law's life during this ministerial transition. Each one was instrumental in a different capacity. If, you haven't already, please, take a moment to remember their varied, but necessary, involvement.

- First, J.T. Pugh helped him with the process of transition. (Before the transition.)
- Second, J.R. Ensey contributed direction in finding the right place to go. (During the transition.)
- Third, V.A. Guidroz opened doors for his financial survival, and prosperity, until the new church was established. (After the transition.)

Because of my father-in-law's story, and now from my own steps of faith, I'm aware of the individuals who have spoken into my own life during similar times. In considering the unique role each one played, I realize that no one person could have accomplished it all, because no individual has all the answers. I've found the wise writer of Proverbs 11:14 to be accurate, *"Where no counsel is, the people fall: but in the multitude of counsellors there is safety."*

The cumulative effort of counselors produces safety. In times of major ministerial transition, this is what we need more than anything else. Search out those voices! And at some point, maybe you'll also experience the same startling reality that I did, when I realized that, because I've lived out a few huge transitions, I'd become someone other ministers now seek out, to gain advice with their own transitions. Over the past few years, I've had numerous conversations with ministers and individuals alike, who were in the midst of transition. It's a real life-altering subject and so important to get it right.

I am so appreciative that Johnny Godair has filled those shoes in my life for over two decades.

WHAT IS THERE TO FEAR?
—J.T. PUGH

ONE OF THE ministers who was a help to my father-in-law was the late, J.T. Pugh. In an indirect way, the same man also greatly impacted my own ministry. Through the years, I heard him speak in large settings, training seminars and recordings, and thankfully, I had personal encounters with him on a number of occasions. Every time he spoke, I walked away deeply impressed, inspired, and informed.

I visited his grave a few years ago in Odessa, Texas. It was on a Pentecost Sunday and I was preaching in the neighboring city of Midland. I mentioned to the pastor, Curtis Benninghoff that I'd like to carve out some time to go find Pastor Pugh's burial place.

I don't often spend time in cemeteries, but it was one place I felt like I had to go, and it was a moving experience for me, because of the life Bro. Pugh lived and the impact he had made on my life and on the apostolic church.

When we found the gravesite, it was not overly impressive, as far as memorials go. In fact, there was someone's grave marker not far from his with the title "Rev. so-and-so." But his unassuming marker simply said "Jesse T." It didn't have the official designation "Reverend" on it at all. It was so understated for such a bigger-than-life individual. But in my opinion, it represented who he was and definitely what he had given his life for.

While being a humble man, he made a huge difference throughout the world in the work of God and deeply affected the lives and futures of many saints, ministers, and leaders. Although he was an indirect mentor to me, he definitely touched my life. My father, my father-in-law, Rev. Pugh, and others like them, convinced me that there would be struggles at every level of transition, but that difficulty should never be a reason to give up or refuse to move forward.

Because he was important to my own ministry, I was curious about how J.T. Pugh handled his own transitions, so I asked a few people who were close to him about that. These were people he purposefully invested in, who were directly influenced by him, and esteemed him greatly.

His own son, Pastor Terry Pugh of Odessa, Texas, said his dad was a master at transition, because he was not afraid of the future. He was always living in the future, and the excitement of tomorrow was greater than the security of today. This is such a departure from many in conventional settings, who play it safe by risking nothing. How amazing it would be to not be afraid of the future.

From the outside, it looked easy for Bro. Pugh to let go and move into the unknown, but I'm confident it was more challenging than what he displayed. But for people who live with such a forward-thinking mindset, tomorrow is not unknown; it is already here. Those viewing the future with apprehension can never truly appreciate this type of living.

One of his sons in the Gospel, Pastor Nathan Scoggins, shared some practical "Pugh" thoughts about transition. From Bro. Pugh's perspective, the process is different for men and women in transition. Pastorally, women have a nesting instinct. Because of this nurturing propensity, they need to be involved throughout the transition and it's a mistake to overlook their maternal feelings and input.

Men, however, have to decrease to relinquish control, like we discussed earlier, when we highlighted John the Baptist. Both Raymond Woodward and J.T. Pugh referenced the concept that John had to decrease at the advancement of Jesus. By doing this, Jesus' ministry increased.

Decreasing cannot take place until release happens. Once you let go, then decrease can occur. This is huge; you should probably read my previous statement again. J.T. Pugh seemed to be able to do this readily. Time and time again, he was able to transition from role to role in the ministry.

Nathan Scoggins also shared that Pastor Pugh mentioned that he would not lead his final pastorate in Odessa, for very long. He was concerned that he'd run out of energy to perform the needed duties of the pastorate. Nathan recalled hearing his pastor say, "I don't want to risk destroying in a few years what has taken me a lifetime to build. I will not let that happen. I will release it to a younger man who's fresh, and ready to take the church to the next level." And that's exactly what he did.

He said it ahead of time, and then he did it. Standing by one's word garners utmost respect by onlookers. Some ministers make bold statements and declarations, but then, when the time comes to carry it out and perform the plan, they're not willing to go through with the transition. Instead they decide they don't see the need for it after all or it isn't the "will" of God, when, it could actually be the issue of personal decrease.

J.T. Pugh did what he said he was going to do. He relinquished the authority and the pastoral role, even though he remained present, still attending the church he once pastored. He was the type of man who could remain in the same city, go to the same church, and not get in the way of the next pastor. He maintained integrity. Nathan said there were many occasions when Bro. Pugh would just tell the people, "You'll have to ask Pastor Terry that question." That's character displayed, nothing more, nothing less.

As a result, Nathan Scoggins reported Brother Pugh often asked himself, "Am I on the right bus? Am I in the right seat? Will I know when it's time to get off the bus?" Knowing when to get off the bus doesn't mean that the journey's over for you. It just means you transition to some other ministerial activity, especially at an older age. Perhaps it's becoming an interim pastor at a church in need of direction or stability, or it could be in some other avenue of ministry, like training, mentorship or writing.

Nathan saw this in the life of Brother Pugh, who went from full-time pastoring of churches to working at our national headquarters, leaving the highest of district leadership roles to preaching around the world and facilitating ministerial roundtable discussions.

But, J.T.'s final earthly transition is perhaps the one that stands out above all others, to many connected to him. It was when he transitioned to the role of being his ailing wife's caregiver. He proved he loved her through this act and his love for her was greater than anything else in the world, including his powerful ministerial calling. Perhaps, that could be the reason both he and Sis. Pugh transitioned from earth to Heaven in the same week.

J.T. Pugh was truly a man to observe and learn from.

V

FACING—AND OVERCOMING— TRANSITION CHALLENGES

In my conversations with multiple pastors who have walked through ministerial transitions, they've shared a couple of challenges that could arise that should be addressed. I won't bring an exhaustive explanation to each of these, but, when you know to watch for these possible situations, you'll be prepared ahead of time.

NEGATIVE CHURCH MEMBERS

DURING A TRANSITION, it's important to acknowledge the strong personalities in a church congregation—especially those attention-demanding people who often rise up and get vocal about what's happening. Considering the past effort and investment placed in them by leadership, they should be supportive, but often they're not, and they can adversely affect other people in the church. It's imperative that both sets of leaders, those who are transitioning out, and those who are transitioning in, to intentionally speak encouragingly about the future of the church and be a voice of reason to innocent people who could get caught up with those vocal, negative ones.

The leader who's transitioning out would do well to call for the people to trust that, before he leaves, he will make sure the church is left in good hands, because, once again, the church and the transition is in the Will of God. If he can't convince them to trust that, then some people will look for opportunities to work against the process of transition. What can be disheartening is when those who often work against the plan are the very people who have consumed the lion's share of the former pastor's concern and energy in the past.

EXITS AND ENTRANCES

SOME PEOPLE in the church stay connected for a long time but decide to leave as soon as a leadership change is presented. I've learned that these kind of exits are an indicator that they were already wanting to leave, but didn't know how to do it, and now, instead of giving the next pastor a chance, they see the transition as the perfect opportunity to leave.

In the smoothest transitions, the former pastor will have advance conversations with the church's influential individuals, key families, and especially those who carry a great responsibility in the church. I would recommend telling them about the decisions being made and let them know they are valued. Sharing highlights will only bring strength to the situation, along with creating buy-in. By all means keep confidential and sensitive information within those who are the final decision-makers.

After operating in this transactional manner, if some choose to still depart, they should be encouraged to leave in a supportive, not destructive manner. If you fail, as the pastor, to let these stakeholders know how much you value their presence and their investment in the church, they will certainly feel lost in the transition's shuffle.

One pastor pointed out how interesting it was to him, how some people in the congregation feel differently when the pastor makes a choice to leave. Some want the pastor to be okay when *they* make decisions to follow the "leading of God" to another place, but they're not as lenient when the pastor feels called elsewhere.

People will not always understand this side of a pastoral change. Sometimes, they perceive the transition as the pastor rudely distancing himself. The former pastor chooses to leave, and the connection, once there between the pastor and the congregation drastically changes. The feeling is awkward, and some individuals get upset. It's easier to blame those stressful emotions on the last leader.

That necessary separation is not rude and it's not distant. In the majority of cases, it's an attempt to be ethical, to make the way smooth for the next pastor to lead effectively. The new pastor will then have liberty to provide a single voice in order to avoid confusion. The uncomfortable disconnect is vital in order to provide the incoming minister opportunity and time to gain influence. It's difficult for both parties, but especially the outgoing pastor. Trust me, I've experienced pastoral transition on both sides.

Transition is harder than expected for many leaders. Sometimes, those who are transitioning in are surprised when people leave. Don't let it catch you off guard. This is a common occurrence. There will always be people who find it a transition to be a convenient time to leave that church. And, truthfully, it's a blessing if those individuals depart in the early stages, especially if they are not willing to get on board. You don't want them to hang around disrupting the new direction, even if keeping them makes it seem like the church is bigger, stronger, and healthier.

Don't waste spiritual or physical energy trying to hold onto people who are determined to go, unless it's a minor misunderstanding or a simple need for pastoral clarity. Why do I say this? Because, just as sure as some individuals will go, there'll be others who will come—simply as a result of the leadership change.

Both ministers and saints encounter pressure during a transition. I believe that, going forward, we can do better with ministerial transitions. Some of the negative situations of the past can be resolved and avoided altogether, just with healthy and constructive dialog. It is my intention to be a continuing voice at this table of transitional improvement and success. There are things we can all learn about the desire of Heaven in each unique change for the local church. Getting it right is the only true option.

SERVING CAN MAKE ALL THE DIFFERENCE

I BELIEVE every Christian is called to a life of religious service. That service is a form of ministry, but it's not the same as the "Five-Fold Ministry," which has to do with particular roles of leadership. The Apostle Paul addressed this by revealing, *"And he gave some, apostles; and some, prophets; and some, evangelists; and some, pastors and teachers."* Ephesians 4:11

The word, "some" is used four times in this single verse. Even though not everyone who names Christ will fall into one of these specific designations, that doesn't devalue the place God has chosen for each individual to minister.

Lisa and I have spent an enormous amount of time, energy, and effort over the past two decades, investing and raising up leaders of various callings. And out of the hundreds of individuals influenced through our deliberate actions, we've found two very specific groups.

One group are those within the body of Christ who have an Ephesians 4:11 "Five-Fold Ministry" selection and anointing. The other group are the men and women who are called to fulfill the many responsibilities of support. Both are vital in the kingdom and, without question, are part of Heaven's divine plan. Pastors do a great injustice to people by not diligently assisting them to find their place of service. And it's important for the pastor to confirm, one way or the other, that place for those sincerely pursuing their purpose. Lingering indefinitely in ministry limbo without approval is exhausting on every level.

Before I share my thoughts about each category, I want to qualify the larger purpose by simply stating that no individual can earn or purchase a place in either group. No person can choose the category in which they would prefer to find fulfillment. These callings find their origins in eternity; reserved for the judgment of the only One who is omniscient. Feeling superior or diminished in either role doesn't enhance the cause. Anointed leaders need to help people find their unique place of service and then help develop them with trust, deliberation, and honesty, working in conjunction with each other.

How can a minister help develop people and their ministries? A few things we have done are:

- hold monthly leadership sessions
- meet in small groups with those pursuing ministry
- spend one-on-one time in strategic conversation
- provide training materials
- travel to conferences as individuals, couples and groups
- enlist the help of other ministers
- discuss and prepare for both the expected and unexpected.

But not one of these things would be of any great value without the discipleship process, preceding the calling or, at least a certain desire for service involvement. Effective ministry is impossible without discipline. I addressed this in my book, *Transition: Life's Unavoidable Reality, A Guide to Successfully Navigating Change.* Adopting the teachings and practices of the one you desire to follow is how that discipleship happens.

In addition to the pulpit and pastoral roles, there are also support roles of ministry within congregations, and discipleship is the avenue leading to those responsibilities.

With Paul and Timothy, it was a pastoral and trainee relationship, which was vitally important, but various scriptures also place importance on individuals within churches who fulfill callings that are not necessarily church planting, a traveling evangelist, a prophetic calling, or a teaching role.

Discipleship on a personal level helps us find those places within the body to serve beyond the platform. Whether we're working in the Five-Fold Ministry or not, people of varying talents, gifts, and passions can still effectively minister within the church body, and this is what everyone committed to Christ should strive for.

I would suggest quickly taking inventory of your Christian experience. Ask yourself these few questions. How far have I come? Have my thoughts and beliefs changed in any way since conversion? Is there a marked growth in my continuing discipleship? What am I serving in today that I never dreamed of, as a new disciple? Am I intentionally walking toward anything specific in kingdom service?

The answers to those questions, undoubtedly, vary from reader to reader and leader to leader, but the truth about where you are, as a willing child of God, will be abundantly clear. No matter which of the specific groups you are destined to, it's important to actively continue to serve—even in the midst of a transition. Setback is never the intention when God is orchestrating the change. It is always about kingdom advancement, personally and collectively.

From my life of transitional ministry, I can unequivocally state, had I not possessed clarity in my calling, abundant trust in the decisions of Heaven, and a determination to stay the course of service, no matter the season or stress, things would not have worked out in the positive ways they have for me. There will never be an acceptable time to cut ties with the work of ministry and expect to continue enjoying the favor of glory.

A heavy dose of reality as it relates to faithful work, comes to us from the words of Jesus in Luke 9:61-62. *"And another also said, Lord, I will follow thee; but let me first go bid them farewell, which are at home at my house. And Jesus said unto him, No man, having put his hand to the plough, and looking back, is fit for the kingdom of God.*

Find your place in kingdom ministry and serve your way through every transition—all the way to that moment when you'll hear the words, "enter in."

VI

A HANDSHAKE IS NOT ENOUGH – AGREEMENTS, LEGALITIES AND TAXES

AGREE TO AGREE

OUTSIDE OF THE personal and spiritual aspects, from which every decision and effort must originate, the practical and legal aspects of a pastoral change is something many never consider.

Many times, ministerial transitions and decisions are left in the hands of clueless people. For some, considering the legal perspectives ventures too far into the carnal and they assume nothing of divine purpose could be accomplished there. Of course, the most important is the divine element! But there's also a natural component in order for the transition to be valid. Solely depending on just one or the other can potentially wreak havoc on a congregation.

It's vitally important to carefully look at all the legal aspects of the church, including the bylaws, how the church is organized with regards to boards, committees, and other leaders, and what the state and governmental laws say regarding the transition, if anything.

A scriptural example to explore is one found in the opening chapter of the book of Acts: *"And in those days Peter stood up in the midst of* the disciples, and said, (the number of names together were about an hundred and twenty,) Men and brethren, this scripture must needs have been fulfilled, which the Holy Ghost by the mouth of David spake before concerning Judas, which was guide to them that took Jesus. For he was numbered with us, and had obtained part of this ministry. Now this man purchased a field with the reward of iniquity; and falling headlong, he burst asunder in the midst, and all his bowels gushed out. And it was known unto all the dwellers at Jerusalem; insomuch as that field is called in their proper tongue, Aceldama, that is to say, The field of blood. For it is written in the book of Psalms, Let his habitation be desolate, and let no man dwell therein: and his bishoprick let another take. Wherefore of these men which have companied with us all the time that the Lord Jesus went in and out among us, Beginning from the baptism of John, unto that same day that he was taken up from us, must one be ordained to be a witness with us of his resurrection. And they appointed two, Joseph called Barsabas, who was surnamed Justus, and Matthias. And they prayed, and said, Thou, Lord, which knowest the hearts of all men, shew whether of these two thou hast chosen, That he may take part of this ministry and apostleship, from which Judas by transgression fell, that he might go to his own place. And they gave forth their lots; and the lot fell upon Matthias; and he was numbered with the eleven apostles." Acts 1:15-26

The selection of Matthias, to take Judas' vacated position as a disciple, took place after the qualifications of two specific men were examined, prayer for guidance concluded, and action was taken by those making this important decision.

So often, I hear of ministers and churches who blatantly ignore their agreed-to bylaws and procedures. Some have no idea what their bylaws even state! Those legalities are strategically put in place, ahead of time, to guide and assist during critical moments. When the legal structure is followed, it removes many unknowns and provides a safety net for all concerned. But when those safeguards are abused, it also affects the spiritual and godly influence of the leaders involved.

Everyone involved should pay close attention to the process, starting with both ministers, plus their families, and then all of the congregants, since there's a lot to gain and a lot to lose during a transition. Following what is spelled out in the official legal documents of the church eliminates the opportunity for opinions and emotions to rule the moment. And that's not the only reason. It's about ethics. When a leader chooses to follow—or disregard— the written guidelines of the church, that speaks to their integrity as a person.

Here are a few of the major things to be consider:

- Will the congregation elect the new pastor, or will the new pastor be appointed by an advisory board with a ratification vote coming from the membership?
- Does the election process happen completely in house, with no outside involvement at all, facilitated by a local board of trustees?
- Will the election be controlled by a district board (made up of preachers) or a distant official board of directors?

Whatever the plan, it's most important to follow the written expectations of the corporate documents.

The truth and often difficult part for people to accept is that the departing minister may be moving on to a greater challenge, to a place where things appear better, and it seems like a win and a benefit to him. That's not necessarily the case, though, if the transition is not handled well and in an above-board manner. In that case, the exiting minister would have a lot to lose, including influence, respect, and appreciation. Not everyone walking this road of ministerial transition readily understands the best way to proceed.

When find yourself involved in a ministerial transition, it's important to do everything you can to assure and maintain a positive and healthy situation, with the ultimate goal of helping those in the church make it to Heaven. This is the bottom line and should never be forgotten in the middle of all the practicalities.

FINANCIAL ARRANGEMENTS AND AGREEMENTS

IN ADDITION to the legal aspects of a transition, it's also important to take a close look at the church's financial strength or lack thereof. Major decisions will need to be made regarding the church's current and future obligations and those finances are a vital part of the church. It's vital that both transitioning ministers have complete openness regarding the church's finances.

First, consider the departing pastor and his family. Will there be a financial obligation or assistance to them? This is especially important if the transition is a result of the former leader's retirement or death.

Then, what about the new pastor? Will the job as pastor be a full time position or will he be expected to be bi-vocational? Will there be any compensation provided from the church?

Further, consideration should also be made regarding those who filled roles and carried responsibilities in the church under the previous leadership. This isn't necessarily a legal thing, but in some cases it could be. Just do the required investigation to find out. Due diligence now can save the new leader stress in the future.

Are there paid staff positions to be aware of? Are there other commitments, outside of the pastoral position, that are bound by contracts or even verbal agreements? Are there end dates that go along with the agreements? Determine if everyone on staff, both paid and volunteer, will keep their present jobs or if the new pastor has the liberty and authority to change, move, adjust, or replace them.

For a smooth transition, these issues must be addressed from the beginning.

These are valid considerations with real potential to either strengthen or diminish the pastor's hand and the church's health in the midst of the transition. And when these types of "nitty-gritty" issues can be worked out, in advance, as part of the transitional arrangements, then the church can move forward more rapidly.

Once again, be certain to cross every "T" and dot every "i" legally, refusing to allow the transition to be a handshake kind of deal. It's even wise to bring some other people into the conversation, which will mean, not only do the two leaders know the intricate details of the agreement, but the board of advisors, elders, families, and the influential people within the congregation will also all be aware of what the agreement is, because the plans and the legalities are clearly spelled out.

Pastor Chase Austin from Houston, Texas, (my nephew), shared this principle with me: "Agreements prevent disagreements." This is true. Make sure everything you can possibly think of is agreed upon in advance. Of course, agreements don't assure that things will be completely easy, going forward, or won't require adjustments, but, at least the advance agreement will prevent some, if not most, of the potential future disagreements.

When I was asked to assume the pastorate of the church with the retiring pastor, I emphatically wanted to create a binding agreement between the two of us. I actively pressed for it to be written out, but the retiring pastor seemed to think a verbal agreement would suffice initially, and the other aspects could be addressed at another time.

I don't recommend this type of arrangement, for several reasons, but in this case, I went forward with the verbal arrangement, because of the mutual level of respect and trust between us. Looking back, however, I would have insisted on our agreements being written, including spelling out the complete transfer of all obligations. One pressing reason for that is because a written agreement can be brought forth if questions ever arise about the particulars of what was agreed upon. Pastoral transitions shouldn't happen as a good ol' boys' handshake; there's too much eternity at stake.

No matter what the situation is, it's important for agreements to be in place for the protection of all concerned.

When money issues arise as the result of a misappropriation of funds, the fallout can be devastating. I recently had a conversation with a pastor who was seriously thinking of resigning his pastorate as a result of the lack of funds. We discussed ways to increase the involvement of those not practicing faithfulness in the area of giving within the congregation. I am happy to report that, after making a concerted effort to involve others, by presenting the reality of lack, the church has experienced rejuvenation in every way, and he is staying. Financial pressures have sidelined so many ministers.

Ambiguous transition agreements often result in unnecessary attacks, questions, and insecurity. Private, secretive, and vague arrangements cause unnecessary assumptions and concerns. Instead, I encourage bringing others into the dialog and coming up with secure, written agreements. That will thwart criticism and provide a safety net for the future.

STRUCTURES AND SYSTEMS: WHAT MATTERS IS RIDING ON THEM

ANOTHER CONSIDERATION for a new pastor is the need to learn about the new church's structures and systems. Every church has a different way of carrying out ministry unique to it.

If you previously pastored, then the structure of any new location will, no doubt, be completely different from the former place and you'll have to figure out how your ministry will fit into the system. The truth is, you don't have experience in that particular place. Things are different there and it will take time to decide out how to marry their previous way of doing things with your way of doing things, hopefully finding an acceptable compromise between the two.

Take this from someone who has years of hands-on experience. The way a church is structured and the systems it has in place will ultimately determine if the church will enjoy steady and continual growth, or not. In fact, it is my top recommendation to any pastor who desires positive results, to carefully look at your current structure and operational systems.

The importance of systems is a priority of my pastoral efforts. For more than a dozen years, I have measured every action taken by how they would complement or enhance our systems. Let me give you a little background so you'll understand why I feel so adamant about a church's systems.

I spent thirty-six months in a learning and a coaching environment, investing thousands of dollars and an enormous number of hours reading, studying, and being held accountable with the intention of mastering this craft. While I don't consider myself a pro, I can say that the focus of all that work has not been in vain. I attribute a tremendous amount of my pastoral accomplishments to the details of carefully crafted structure and systems.

One lamenting pastor pointed this next dilemma out to me, when I asked him about his recent transition. He said, "I've realized we don't always have experience leading a congregation of a different size from where we were previously—whether the number is larger or smaller. In a transition from a larger congregation to a smaller one, you might think that because there are fewer individuals involved, it will be easier. But, that's not always the case, because you will undoubtedly have fewer resources, fewer volunteers, and less financial support for the work."

He had a good point. One positive thing I've encountered, when a congregation is smaller, numerically, is that, in certain situations, you can see positive changes happen much quicker than when you're trying to redirect a larger church. People often say, "It takes a long time to turn a ship." It's not impossible, but it's definitely more challenging, because moving abruptly has the potential to capsize the vessel and destroy the purpose.

On the other hand, if you formerly pastored in a smaller congregation and are transitioning into a larger one, trust me, you'll have to step up every part of your game to meet the demands of the bigger congregation. Just because you successfully managed a handful doesn't mean you can automatically handle hundreds, or even thousands.

There's a tremendous amount of growth necessary within the individual in both situations and no one but you can put in the effort to see it accomplished. You and I are solely responsible for our own progress. Excuses are just a cop-out used by those who are lazy and unmotivated.

In order to stay accurate with the scripture, which states, *"...thou hast been faithful over a few things, I will make thee ruler over many things...,"* please note that this is a divine advancement. Matthew 25:21, 23.

The only One who can help us make up for the obvious and undetected deficits is the Lord. When He takes control, a great amount of ground can be made up in a short span of time. But don't miss the faithfulness part. Being faithful in this context, in no way, suggests being inactive, but, instead, it actually means achieving everything possible with what one has been given. So, if you are not seeing what God promised come to pass, perhaps the delay is because you haven't intentionally pursued personal growth. You are failing to seek out avenues to be equipped for the task ahead. And, by the way, just because you've been in a specific location for an exaggerated length of time doesn't necessarily merit the designation of "faithful"—from my interpretation of scripture.

Chances are, you buried what God blessed you with long ago, by playing it safe and taking no risks. Often the lack of progress in every area of the church; evangelistically, financially, and in the development of spiritually-mature Christian growth, is simply a blatant lack of work. Preaching new sermons and revelations every time you mount the pulpit is not the solution to every congregational need and Heaven-ordained mandate.

It's imperative to investigate everything about the church structure closely, understanding fully that it's impossible to truly know how it's all going to come together. People are different, cultures are different, finances are different, and even stability can be different. And, of course, without divine intervention; nothing will ever seamlessly come together, no matter what a person's intellect, experience, understanding, or effort.

Even when all the details are studied in advance and the best possible plans are set up, things can still be misrepresented, poorly communicated, or viewed completely differently from the former leader to the next. Plus, what one pastor or leader can tolerate, the next may not be able to deal with.

From conversations I've had with people who have recently gone through pastoral change, it's important to go into it with your eyes wide open, not expecting it to be one particular way, when all the evidence, and all of the examples, and all of the reality points to something different. Most likely, your specific situation—at least in the early days—isn't going to be a whole lot different than the last person.

My suggestion is to prepare in advance for the uniqueness of the challenge, and instead of shrinking away from it, rise to the occasion, realizing you're able to face it and win, with Heaven's assistance.

In the long run, the investment, the time, and the energy will all pay off, even if, upfront, when you're working through all these challenges, it doesn't feel like it. Truthfully, it can be more stressful in a new situation than what you thought it was going to be, and you'll have a lot less return than what you anticipated. This has everything to do with the fact that influence takes time to develop and it can't be forced.

In times like these, when the pressure is on and everything seems to be moving at a snail's pace, the past can suddenly look really inviting and you can be tempted to rethink your position. Let me remind you that yesterday didn't look as inviting when it was the present.

WHAT DOES THE LAW SAY ABOUT TRANSITIONS?

NO DISCUSSION of pastoral transitions would be complete without hearing from those who not only understand the spiritual implications but also the legal considerations of the transition. I asked two minister friends who each have dual professions—one as a lawyer and the other as a tax accountant—to speak to this subject. I asked them what the church and the two pastors should be aware of with a transition.

My friend, Rev. Ronald Dean Ingle, Jr. shared his thoughts about ministerial transitions from the perspective of being both a pastor and an attorney:

> Pastoral transition is fraught with traps and snares for the unwary or the unprepared minister and church body. It is imperative (morally, ethically, and legally) that any pastoral transition is done above reproach and in the light. To handle pastoral transition the correct way is a great testimony both to the believer and the non-believer. To do otherwise can and will

bring reproach to the local church, as well as to the work of the Lord in general.

The "old school" way of running a church from the proverbial "front pocket" is outdated and invites confusion. It also invites trouble with legal authorities, as well as lawsuits from anyone who feels slighted. The United States Supreme Court has ruled that our courts generally do not get involved in "ecclesiastical matters" except when it involves property. Our courts usually will refrain from disputes over policy or personality conflicts. Churches are expected to police themselves in some sense. The best way to do that is to make sure a church's bylaws are airtight. Of course, there are exceptions to everything, and a court could get involved in situations such as:

- An aggrieved staff member could bring an action for breach of his or her contract, if the church breached the contract and the staff member incurred monetary damages.
- Marriages at the church—Who can get married on the church property and who is authorized to perform the wedding? If it is not clearly spelled out in the bylaws that non-church members cannot get married at the respective church facility, then that church has invited a discrimination lawsuit.

"Back in the day," pastoral transition usually consisted of the senior pastor bringing in the new pastor and expecting everyone to approve. That doesn't work so well these days because some parishioners are conflicted, as they may be very loyal to the senior pastor, but, be uneasy for any number of reasons, about the new pastor.

The "best" way for pastoral transition is modeled by our political system: let the voting body decide. Of course, this will invite some sense of politicking, but the parishioners will feel they had some say in the decision. The church bylaws should reflect a process by which any new pastor will be selected. I would also suggest a clause in the bylaws that allows for the senior pastor to step back in (if they so desire) in the event of moral, financial, or spiritual failure, or untimely death of the new pastor. This process would protect the senior pastor's years of work and service, but also give the new pastor an opportunity to develop into their role.

A church should also make sure it is up-to-date with all requisite annual resolutions, bylaws, state or local filings, policies, etc. in place. A church body will want to make sure that their bylaws clearly spell out a timeline for any pastoral transition, as well as a remuneration schedule (salary or percentage of the tithing), who handles the church finances, who handles counseling of parishioners, who runs the office on a day to day basis, among a plethora of specific concerns.

As I write this, I am involved in a matter wherein a long-term pastor (over four decades with the same church), just retired with a clear expectation of the church to pay him a monthly retirement benefit. The new pastor was screened by the board and the church approved all details of the pastoral transition several years ago. Everyone was aware of the details and felt comfortable about the way their pastor would be cared for. The new pastor now refuses to honor the agreement. The retired pastor is suffering financially, as he was planning on the promised income. Of course, for every bad situation, there are many churches that have things in order and the new pastor honors the documents voted on by the church (retirement packages, fade-out agreements, etc.). Those instances are refreshing.

I have also represented churches which did not have proper resolutions, bylaws, state or local filings, policies, etc. in place. These situations are frustrating because anyone can enter the fray at the last minute and claim to be a member, claim to have an interest in the church property, or claim to have the ability to vote on major decisions. It is difficult for a District or Executive official to step in and totally understand the lay of the land.

If I had to choose, I would always choose to engage in a matter where there is a clear understanding of what the voting body of the church intended.

A church must take the time to set themselves up correctly. If the founding pastor failed to do so, the new pastor must. If a church is an approved non-profit entity, then they are required to protect all assets (real estate, facilities, funds, and personal property such as sound equipment, pews, chairs, furnishing, fixtures, etc.). In the event of dissolution of the church, all non-profits are required to disburse their assets to other non-profits. To do otherwise invites the wrath of the Internal Revenue Service and scrutiny on anyone who may have benefitted from the improper disbursement of church assets.

Recently a pastor of a large church in a metropolitan area was imprisoned (along with his wife) for taking almost all church income for himself. If a church does not operate above reproach and in a legal manner, they stand the risk of losing their non-profit status. If this happens, not only do parishioners lose the ability to take church contributions as a tax write off, it also makes an exciting story for the local news outlets.

WHAT ABOUT THE IRS?

CHURCH TRANSITIONS HAVE tax implications as well, and my friend, Rev. Donald Meade, Sr., retired pastor and public accountant, (specializing in clergy and church tax accounting procedures), spoke to that:

> Each of the three parties, (the outgoing pastor, the incoming pastor, and the church itself) have specific legal and tax implications that should be considered before, during and after the transition.

The Church

First, I hope that the church has already been operating according to bylaws that are set up in compliance with the 501 (C) 3 IRS tax exempt status for not-for-profit religious organizations. The bylaws are the most important document for a church, as it relates to the U.S. government. One requirement of that compliance is to have the local church government organized in one of these three most common ways:

- *Corporate Qualified Congregational Government*: This type of church government is set up so that every qualified member of the church has the right to vote.
- *Limited Qualified Corporate Government*: In this form, the voting rights are spelled out in the bylaws.
- *Corporate Board of Directors Government*—This third type of church has a board of directors who make all the corporate decisions and the congregation only has the right to ratify, with a yes or no vote, a decision presented by the board.

The type of church government in the church's bylaws will determine how the transition to a new pastor will be handled so it's imperative that the bylaws are well-written and then, when the time comes, they should be followed. The bylaws are a legal document recognized by the Federal and State government.

The Incoming Pastor

When you pick up your car from the auto repair shop at the end of the workday, many times you experience what our family calls the "five o'clock shock" (realizing the repair is going to cost way more than you expected). It's important that the incoming pastor doesn't experience that same type of shock when he learns about all the church's financial responsibilities.

Information about every financial motion, resolution or contract that the board has put in place, prior to the selection of a candidate for pastor needs to be shared with the new pastor—ideally before the final transition happens. Often, those financial obligations include providing monetary support for the former pastor and his family—especially if they're in retirement age.

The incoming pastor needs to understand both the church's financial obligations and where the funds will come from, to pay for those obligations. Obviously, it depends on the size of the church and the money that's available, but in most cases, those funds come from the tithing account. If the new pastor will also be paid from that same tithing account, the church's obligations could affect his compensation, so prior to the transition, the board and the new pastor should agree on a plan for the new pastor's pay.

All pastors should be set up as a W-2 employee of the church (NOT as an independent contractor 1099 or Schedule C). Ministers have dual status recognition with the IRS: they're "employees" for income tax purposes, but "self-employed" for FICA and Medicare purposes. And ministers should educate themselves about whether or not they should take the option, that's only available for clergy, of not withholding taxes from their pay. Always get professional help so it's all done correctly!

Finally, I recommend that the incoming pastor get an employment agreement from the church that spells out both his responsibilities and his benefits. That way, no one will be concerned that he's deciding all that for himself; instead, it's an agreement, made in advance.

The Outgoing Pastor

If the outgoing pastor is transitioning to a new church that will be compensating him in the future, the past church generally has less of an obligation to provide for him after he moves on, although in some cases, there are transitional severance moneys provided. However, in the case of a retirement from active ministerial duties, most churches have set up a plan to support him (as well as his wife, after his death). So that there's no miscommunication between the former and the new pastor, all that should be set in writing and freely shared.

Before the transition, (ideally, this should be in place well before a transition is considered), the board should decide, in advance, and the new pastor should understand:

- How much will be paid to the former pastor
- Whether it's a percentage or a fixed amount
- Where those funds will come from
- How long it will be paid (a specific time frame or until death?)
- Whether the widow of the former pastor will receive it until her death

Often, the support will include a retirement payment plan and a housing allowance, and both of those types of support have tax considerations:

- *Retirement Income*—The church should issue the former pastor a 1099-R (retirement) form indicating how much was paid. The former pastor will pay Federal and State taxes on this income, but not self employment taxes (FICA and Medicare).
- *Housing Allowance*—The IRS rules for establishing an approved housing allowance must be followed. The church does not put this income on a federal form. Instead they would just provide a letter stating how much was given to the former pastor for housing. In the case of this allowance, no Federal or State taxes are owed, but FICA and Medicare are due.

It's so important for the outgoing pastor to consult a tax professional, (who understands the laws regarding retiring ministers), to advise about what percentage of the money should be allocated as retirement income and what percentage should be considered housing allowance. That way, the retired pastor will have the best possible strategy for his taxes.

Before a transition

Wise and responsible pastors and church boards understand that a transition will be coming at some point in the future—if not due to retirement, then due to death. It's so important to seek out a tax professional, ahead of time, who understands and specializes in the clergy benefits of the IRS code to educate them on these issues. Not all CPA'S know the clergy rules.

Then, they should work together to put something in place in the corporate minutes of the church, well in advance of a retirement or an emergency, so the church and the pastor's family will be cared for. Make sure there's a life insurance policy that will provide enough for the wife's future. Make sure the church is incorporated. Make sure the bylaws are well-written and then followed. Do all the work in advance so that, when transition time comes, it will go as smoothly as possible.

CONSIDER THE TIMING

TIMING IS, perhaps, the most important aspect of the entire transitional process. The intricate details can't be overdone. Doing the wrong thing at the right time never works out. Neither does doing the right thing at the wrong time.

I am a massive proponent of the necessity of deliberately creating wins in the initial stages of a major transition. It's imperative to be sensitive to how things are playing out and extremely intentional about all the timing issues. Wins breed more wins, and, in the process, attraction transpires, excitement is enhanced, and support builds. The opposite happens when mistakes are made and losses are incurred.

If you know a pastoral change is coming, I say this with ultimate emphasis, prepare, prepare, prepare!

Start by preparing yourself in every possible way: Focus on the mental, spiritual, and emotional components contained within the upcoming journey. Trust me, each of those will weigh greatly in the success or failure of the transition.

Don't stop with yourself. Next, work to prepare those closest to you. Prepare your family, because they will also be directly affected by the transition. You'll absolutely want to spend time in open conversation with them, going over the details. Their input, insight, and involvement will make the future challenges more palatable.

Once you've prepared yourself and your family, don't neglect the pastoral responsibility to prepare the church—first through intentional preaching and then through direct, face-to-face communication. This happens by addressing smaller groups and having conversations with influential individuals, often considered the stakeholders (i.e. boards, committees, leadership teams, major contributors of finance, prayer coordinators, and those actively involved).

I recommend starting with presenting the big picture of apostolic succession, and like previously mentioned, the individual's connection to the Lord, to the truth, and to the local church.

I stress again, timing is a huge factor but in regards to the congregation, communication is the one non-negotiable. Suggest abundantly that they should give the next pastor a chance, because this is their church and they need to stay connected. Remind people they're not just there because of a previous pastor, his personality or charisma, although these things may have initially been the reason. There is much more involved now. What keeps people connected to a particular church family is an unwavering commitment to God and where He has planted them.

Before the transition even comes, the pastor should be communicating to the congregation that each one of them are there for reasons beyond just their connection with the current leadership. When people are floundering in moments of change, promote, promote, promote the bigger purpose. The ultimate goal is a true walk with God. A close second is a passionate investment in the unchurched community and sincere ministry within the body.

Help them recall the necessary part they have played in these things. People can quickly forget why they are at the church. It's because they love God, love the truth, and because they have friends there. Consider mentioning each of these things.

Minister and saint alike need to be constantly reminded that the key purpose of ministry transition is so the church can powerfully and effectively continue, thus, moving the kingdom forward. It's absolutely necessary we get it right because if we don't, then precious humanity can potentially find themselves lost in the shuffle of change.

One pastor said, "I've heard people describe it as passing the test of time—like making the most of each season while you're in it. You have a certain season to raise your kids. You have a certain season to build a career. Eventually, those windows close, so it's what you do while the windows are open that is important, and also being aware of when windows are closing."

Work to understand the aspects of time and how they play into a transition. I heard J.T. Pugh say that the common denominator among successful people, both in and out of the church, was a sense of timing. Getting the timing of transition correct, matters.

Ecclesiastes 3:1 says, *"To every thing there is a season, and a time to every purpose under the heaven."* Time has a direct tie to purpose. We emphasize purpose so much, but often fail to elevate the importance that timing plays into achieving that purpose. In further reference to this verse we can extrapolate that the word, "seasons" indicates a defined start time and finish. To process this in the light of successful purpose, consider the following.

Success is defined differently for people in the varying situations of life. What's vital as it relates ministerial transition is an understanding of what God considers ministerial success to be.

Often, in religious circles, people believe a successful ministry is one where the minister holds a single position, such as a pastorate, and that position is meant to last throughout the holder's lifetime—even though the Bible doesn't specifically teach that. Evidence of another truth is found in the above scriptural reference, *"there is a season, and a time."* The timeframe expected for a minister to effectively serve is different for different people. Seasons are different lengths in different situations. Even in the natural, that's true. I was raised in Texas where the summers lasted forever—or at least they seemed to. Here in Colorado, where I live now, winter drags on forever and summer barely shows up before it's gone. The length of a season varies, based on the circumstance.

Something intriguing to consider is found in Numbers 4. The men of Kohath, Gershon, and Merari were chosen to serve in the tabernacle—but with one qualifying factor. They had to be between the ages of thirty and fifty.

Numbers 4:1-3, 22-23, 29-30:

"And the Lord spake unto Moses and unto Aaron, saying, Take the sum of the sons of Kohath from among the sons of Levi, after their families, by the house of their fathers, From thirty years old and upward even until fifty years old, all that enter into the host, to do the work in the tabernacle of the congregation.

Take also the sum of the sons of Gershon, throughout the houses of their fathers, by their families; From thirty years old and upward until fifty years old shalt thou number them; all that enter in to perform the service, to do the work in the tabernacle of the congregation.

As for the sons of Merari, thou shalt number them after their families, by the house of their fathers; From thirty years old and upward even unto fifty years old shalt thou number them, every one that entereth into the service, to do the work of the tabernacle of the congregation."

They worked on a specific responsibility during a specific season of their life. We know they were of the Levitical priesthood, called of God, chosen by God, appointed to do the work of God in connection with the Tent of Meeting.

Please don't miss this; they were handling the set up and representation of holy things. They were serving, bearing burdens, and handling incredible responsibility with importance impossible to accurately describe. But this was only in a certain season of their lives—a specific responsibility for a specific length of time. This concept has been lost or simply forsaken in modern ecclesiastical times.

There's something positive to be said about people who know their calling—including its timing—and operate within those boundaries. In my opinion, this is an absent piece of understanding in this current generation. For the men of Numbers 4, twenty years of faithfulness marked success.

I wholeheartedly believe what God desires with every season of ministry, is for both the church and the minister to continue on, without fallout, substantial loss, or setbacks that can years to overcome. (Sadly, some churches and ministers never rebound after going through a difficult transition.)

When you're the incoming leader, here is valuable advice: Give people time to adjust to the news and time to process the shock before moving forward too aggressively with wide-sweeping changes, but don't delay in providing direction, once God has spoken clearly to you.

And to the outgoing leader, I share what Ron Liles, a now retired minister from Texas stated to a close friend of mine, "You're only as good as your last performance." Remember, when you resign and move on, you're not the only one dealing with the transition. So are people in the church. You may think you have a lot of influence left, but once you leave, influence diminishes, which is okay, because the next pastor needs to be able to step into that influential role.

Ministerial change is not easy, but everyone can get through it and, in the end, the church, the minster, and the minster's family can look back with joy, knowing that God was in control and His purpose was accomplished. If this truly is the case, then, people will stay connected to the church and continue to grow beyond the leadership of the previous pastor.

When a pastoral transition is healthy, neither the surrounding community nor the leadership of the church is harmfully affected. The plan of God is recognized and fulfilled, and Heaven receives all of the glory. If the heart of the previous pastor is right, then the church's future success, without that former pastor's continuing influence, is a testimony of the effective investment he made in it.

We briefly talked about the ideal state of the church, before, during, and after a transition, but is this typical? The sad reality is, not always. The goal, of course, is for both the church and the ministers involved to come out of a transition both better and stronger. But, from my personal experience, that doesn't always happen.

It was good for us when we left our first church plant in Asheville, North Carolina and it was good for the congregation, but it was extremely challenging where I was headed. I've experienced it both ways: good leaving and hard going in, and vice versa.

WORKING TOGETHER

HAVING time to prepare for a transition is ideal, if you know the change is coming. However, in certain circumstances, such as the sudden death of the previous pastor, or other unfortunate circumstances, you don't know a transition is coming ahead of time. In that case, I believe, (as do the other ministers I interviewed, before writing this book), that the transition should be handled as quickly and cleanly as possible.

Don't drag it out simply because the transition came as a surprise. Stringing pastoral transition out over extended periods of time, in most circumstances, will affect the church negatively. Just take my word for it! I've heard many stories of extensive loss, when the timing is drawn out.

This may be a taboo conversation for some in the religious world, but I feel a brief explanation is necessary. If the transition is happening as a result of a moral failure in the leadership, the entire process is hard for everyone involved. There's no way around that. So, expect the selection process to be a bit slower. And, throughout that transition, be as open and as consistent with communication as possible, answering as many of the congregation's questions as is appropriate; don't leave them wondering.

Other circumstances that become challenging times are poor financial and pastoral decisions and actions. These types of situations affect everyone involved. We should strive to keep the church and its leaders in a good light and good standing in the community.

But invest considerably less effort into attempting to please people who have no skin in the game. The old adage that says, "If you try to please everyone, you will end up pleasing no one," really applies here! The leadership should determine timeframes of change, not parishioners.

Some folks are nothing more than a distraction. Just ask Nehemiah about Sanballat, Tobiah, and Geshem.

Nehemiah 6:1-3

"Now it came to pass when Sanballat, and Tobiah, and Geshem the Arabian, and the rest of our enemies, heard that I had builded the wall, and that there was no breach left therein; (though at that time I had not set up the doors upon the gates;) That Sanballat and Geshem sent unto me, saying, Come, let us meet together in some one of the villages in the plain of Ono. But they thought to do me mischief. And I sent messengers unto them, saying, I am doing a great work, so that I cannot come down: why should the work cease, whilst I leave it, and come down to you?"

In most cases, a good transition happens rather quickly—at least the part the congregation sees. Many times, it's announced in a service one week, and the next pastor or potential leader is introduced and voted on or ratified within a few weeks after. Believe me, this sort of timeline isn't uncommon and in the majority of situations, it's probably one of the healthier ways to go about it. I know opinions abound and they are a dime a dozen. Since, I'm the one writing this book, this one is mine.

When there's a long lapse of leadership with no one to direct the church, people begin to feel distressed and disgruntled inadvertently allowing trouble to rise. Often, the transition has a two-pronged approach and that's okay.

The business and the administrative side may take longer to iron out all the details and particulars, but the pulpit responsibility, and the visionary responsibility should typically happen rather quickly. That way, the congregation isn't left to flounder without a leader while the legalities are being worked out.

Several pastors I interviewed stressed the importance of creating a plan and then doing everything in your power to stick with it. If the plan is to resign one week and have someone there in the next week or within two weeks, then follow through with that plan. Don't change in the middle. It causes confusion and things can become even more challenging.

Usually the people who are behind the challenges are the ones who will get vocal. One minister shared with me how surprised he was by which of the people who didn't handle the transition well. There are moments when the ones who should be on board, are not, and the ones you would never expect to support a move like this, are.

Openly presenting the pertinent business details with the congregation, and sticking closely to the announced plan, can go a long way toward smoothing out those challenges. I'm not certain where I first heard the statement, "We are often down on the things we are not up on," but it is so true.

As you have realized, a plethora of plans need to be made before transition happens, but for the resigning pastor, once it's over, and the plans are complete, don't get involved after the fact, unless the new pastor asks you for input. Ideally, strive to make the transition final, act on it quickly, and be done.

When my father-in-law resigned his church in Missouri, he announced it one service and the next pastor was there the following service. That's fast! Just be aware that, even if it's done quickly, (which in my opinion, is the best way), it's still hard for the congregation because they're in shock and don't feel ready or prepared for something to happen that swiftly.

I stated previously that a former pastor should intentionally disconnect from the church. Now let me address the other side of the coin. From my observation, churches can experience an unnecessary setback when the incoming leaders are not willing or not open to get behind-the-scenes input from the previous pastor. The truth is if he was engaged and cared about the vision, he can provide a wealth of knowledge to the new pastor and help support his success.

Why are we so adamant about starting over again on our own, when, instead, we can really gain strength and understanding from the previous generation's wisdom and not have to try to face this vital transition alone. Even in the best of circumstances, there will be setbacks contained in every ministerial change and I learned from my own mentors to expect those tumultuous moments. As a result of their advice, I was prepared for those times and refused to let any resistance derail the necessary transition from transpiring.

If the situation and people involved are supportive, the former pastor should stay connected to the incoming pastor, at least for a season, after the transition has happened, for the sake of the congregation and the direction it has embraced. Both ministers want what's best for the church so when they work together, as one is leaving and the other is arriving, they can minimize the loss of ground and spiritual heights that have been previously gained. How does it help the congregation if, when a new person assumes the helm of a particular church, they are oblivious of the history of the church and its people? How much better it would be to allow—even welcome—the former pastor to offer his understanding, insight, purpose, and reasoning gained from carrying a burden for this local church for the time he was the pastor?

Wise leaders learn from the ups and downs of yesterday. Living as though it didn't happen is a mistake. Too many incoming pastors deal with unnecessary struggles because they don't make use of the knowledge of the one person who really knows the church's story.

Don't allow arrogance to work its way into the transition. Asking every possible question of the previous leader only enhances your ability to lead, instead of having to start over to learn the hard way. Pastor Jesse Williams and I had many meaningful and enlightening conversations which helped me tremendously and his insight was the confirmation I needed to make the necessary changes.

As the former leader, you know the people who make up the congregation, even though you've transitioned out of that leadership role. You've carried a burden for them individually, providing the direction for the church, for years. You can greatly benefit the next person and contribute invaluable wisdom to assist the future growth of the church.

These things will only happen if you continue to provide a welcoming and transparent voice to the new leader. If there's no connection at all and you're completely distant or removed from the situation, then the learning curve will be much greater for the incoming pastor and it will take an enormous amount of time for him to come to grips with the intricate details of leading the new church.

Remember, regarding ethics, that it's necessary to distance yourself from the people, so they will not indefinitely look at you as their leader, but it doesn't mean you have to be absent from the life of the new leader. You can continue to be an invaluable, behind-the-scenes resource for him. For a while, he will be endeavoring to find and secure his pastoral footing, figuring out the direction, and current state of the church. The former pastor, unquestionably, knows and is able to communicate things to greatly help the new pastor, if allowed to speak to the ongoing process.

Sometimes the circumstances make it impossible to use the former pastor as an advisor. In that case, it's important to connect with those who've gone through a similar situation. That way, you will not need to recreate the wheel. Remember, you were not meant to do this alone, so, talk to people who have been down the road, find out what they learned, and what they wish would have been different.

It is a great disadvantage when an incoming pastor has no clue where the church is, on various levels. But, how can he learn what he needs to know unless it is thoroughly communicated by the exiting leader or someone closely connected to the inner workings of that particular body. Not knowing the strengths or weakness are —or more importantly, what the next steps should—be can be daunting. Just ask anyone who has experienced it! My advice to an incoming pastor? Focus primarily on this discovery process before moving on to anything else. Once that happens, then divine direction can be realized, internalized, and adopted.

Okay, let me get real. Get help if you need it. For some ministers, pride will not allow them to ask the necessary questions or admit they're not sure, they're unclear or they don't have all the answers. What a waste!

And to the departing leader? His hands shouldn't be so full of working in the new assignment that he refuses available time for the previous one. Just because he's found purpose in the next phase of ministry doesn't mean he should turn his back on the last effort. Ideally, both the former and the new pastor should determine to openly communicate with each other so that some difficulties can be alleviated, if not avoided completely, and the church can continue to grow in a healthy manner.

Before, during, and even after the transition, there should be sincere and helpful dialogue between the previous and new leaders, the emphasis of which should be regarding the people, and where they are seeking growth in Christ. Additionally, there should be honest sharing about potential situations which could negatively affect future progress. The ongoing success of the church and kingdom advancement matters more than secrets or personal agendas. Why hinder divine purpose when you can enhance it?

Unexpected things will certainly come and the one way to lessen their impact is to have an extremely detailed timeline of transitional events and expectations recorded upfront. Then follow the plan.

FROM TRANSITION TO TRANSFORMATION: SELL OUT TO THE PROCESS

I READ SOMETHING a couple of years ago, from Virtual Coach, Eben Pagan, who wrote about the difference between transition and transformation. We haven't talked about this in depth, but here at the end of the book, I want to bring it to light.

Eben Pagan described the difference between the two like this: "In considering a flight of stairs, transition is one step in the staircase. Transformation is the entire staircase." With transition, you take the first step, and then the next and the next—one step at a time. No matter how many steps there are, you're taking one step at a time. That's transition. Each time, you just take the next obvious step, whatever that step is, for you. You can't skip over three or four steps and continue to be effective. Remember, one step after another.

So, for you, what is your next step? I challenge you to simply take it! Determine, before reading another word, to intentionally do it right now. Then, when you've ascended the entire flight of stairs and look back, you'll suddenly realize you've experienced transformation. Pagan says every transition is ultimately leading us closer to transformation, and I agree. Reaching the top must be the goal.

Again, this idea goes back to my first book, *Transition: Life's Unavoidable Reality, A Guide to Successfully Navigating Change,* where I maintain that all of our transitions in life lead us to the most important one of all, which is transformation from this life to the next.

From a practical perspective, Pagan says transitions in life can take three to six months while transformations normally take six months to three years. Transformation doesn't happen immediately, or even quickly. Instead, it takes time to get through all the transitional steps. In the end, though, it'll be worth it.

It's so important to believe in the process and sell out to it. 1 John 3:2 says, *"Beloved, now are we the sons of God, and it doth not yet appear what we shall be: but we know that, when he shall appear, we shall be like him; for we shall see him as he is."* Our prevailing goal then, is to be like the Lord. The transitions we're going through here and now will lead us to that final one, the one with eternal consequences.

I was recently introduced to seven keys for a positive transition, by Pastor Kevin Gerald from the state of Washington and I'd like to offer his guidelines to you. If you're interested, you can view them on my website: https://www.robertmitchell2.com/keys/

CONCLUSION—WHAT'S THE BOTTOM LINE?

SO MANY CHURCHES experience the death of progress. They experience decline, a loss of vision, and a loss of purpose, productivity, and effectiveness. In the process, we must be reminded and even forced, if necessary, to realize that this is God's church. His church is much bigger than our own personal agendas and we need to be willing to relinquish whatever individual attachments we possess for the progress and future of the church.

What does it boil down to? It's about the all-encompassing eternal souls of the people. My friend, Pastor Jerry Dean, from Bossier City, Louisiana, calls it "the crushing weight of eternity." It's an unrelenting burden which causes you to pray incisively, labor to be sensitive, and press forward, attempting to do what's right and necessary in every transitional situation.

We must never forget that He's getting a bride ready and it requires a lot of work for a bride to prepare for her wedding. She has to find the right dress, a perfect location for the ceremony, and then make many decisions about every aspect of the occasion, before that big day arrives. A personal friend was married recently, and he shared with me a few weeks before the event that, from his male perspective, he was ready for all the preparations to be over. Interestingly, the entire time he was thinking that way, his bride was working tirelessly on all the details, hoping everything would come together the exact way she wanted and had dreamed of.

John wrote in Revelation 19:7, *"Let us be glad and rejoice, and give honour to him: for the marriage of the Lamb is come, and his wife hath made herself ready."*

In a similar way, Pastors also have a responsibility to help get a bride (the church) ready. The pastor in transition should not hinder the work or stop the progress of the church, but to transition in the most healthy and productive way possible. Holding on to a church or ministry past one's ordination, circumvents the greater desire of Heaven.

In some situations, this means the previous pastor must relinquish authority and control, even though it seems impossible. It means giving the next generation of leaders, the community, and the world, a chance to live out their lives just like earlier generations did. It's about the contemporary and coming generation creating their own history.

In my opinion, it's an injustice to continue leading or controlling without allowing for change. Many people fall into the trap of thinking they're leading even though Godly and effective change never comes. It doesn't honor the previous generation of leaders to just repeat exactly or simply maintain what they did. The new leader should wholeheartedly strive to build on what the former pastor established, and then taking the work and effort to the next level.

Author George Hunter said, "We do not honor our founders by

blindly perpetuating in a changing world what they once did. We honor them by doing for our time and culture what they did for theirs!"

YOU DON'T HAVE TO FACE MINISTRY TRANSITIONS ALONE...

At the request of many of my readers, I've created an **online course and mentorship program** that goes deeper into the content that I covered in this book.

One of the secrets to successfully navigating a Ministry Transition is support. Not only have I seen how vital mentorship is firsthand in my journey, but my clients have shared with me how much easier the transition can be with a comforting hand on your shoulder.

To learn more and sign up, visit:
https://www.robertmitchell2.com/mt-course

ACKNOWLEDGMENTS

No project like this can be accomplished without help from others and, although there's no way to list everyone who was instrumental in this project, I do want to thank a few key people.

Thanks to my many friends and ministers who allowed me to ask a few probing questions while researching this book:

- Chase Austin
- Johnny Godair
- Darryl Hooper
- Eric Ingle
- Scott Leitner
- Jonathan Barley
- Terry Pugh
- Nathan Scoggins
- Raymond Woodward

When you need the knowledge of professionals, it's great to have associates you can ask. I'm thankful for these two men who provided their legal and tax expertise, specifically directed towards those facing a ministerial transition:

- Ronald Ingle, Pastor and Attorney
- Donald Meade, retired Pastor and Public Accountant

I'm thankful for the writing support I received from the Self Publishing School (https://xe172.isrefer.com/go/affegwebinar/RobertMitchell2/) and The Jim Edwards Method (https://ebookcoach.zaxaa.com/a/5471726549563).

Additional thanks to:

The extraordinary fellow author Joy Haney for taking time from her busy schedule to write the forward of this book.

Angelique Mroczka, for the print and kindle version layout and formatting. Along with the technical work, she provides friendly advice and expertise in all areas of authorship. It was great working together again.

Keidi Keating, for additional editing and input.

Angie Alaya for the excellent cover and back design work. A gem found on Fiverr.

Karen Hemmes, for the extensive rewrite, organization, and editing. The final version is so much better. Two books down and several more to go!

All the early readers for pointing out the minor flaws and providing supportive endorsements.

And last, but not least, my Savior, Jesus Christ, the Only God.

ABOUT THE AUTHOR

Prolific speaker, minister, church planter, husband, father, author, and adventurer, Robert Mitchell writes about transitions from a wealth of personal life experiences. His first book, *Transition: Life's Unavoidable Reality*, released in 2016.

Robert was born in Houston, Texas, and raised in a home filled with love, acceptance, encouragement, and vision. He has lived in five states, visited every state, major city, many national parks and notable landmarks in the United States, and traveled throughout the Americas, Europe, Asia, and the Middle East. He has spoken or facilitated in over 10,000 events with audiences from one to thousands, in a variety of venues.

Robert holds a Master's Degree in Leadership. Continually reading, learning, and investing in ongoing personal development, he has taught, coached, lead, advised, and given guidance to hundreds of individuals through the changes and obstacles they've faced.

Robert's ministry passion is in evangelism and church planting, having personally started three works and mentoring other leaders in additional new ministries. Robert and his wife Lisa currently live in Colorado, where he pastors two startup churches. He and Lisa are parents to three daughters.

For more information, please visit: http://www.robertmitchell2.com

Social media whereabouts:

Twitter: @RobertMitchell2

Facebook: Robert Mitchell II

LinkedIn: Robert Mitchell

Made in the USA
Columbia, SC
22 December 2019

85620911R10093